SYMBOLS

Lines

 Valley fold, front fold

Arrows

 Bend in that direction.

 Folding and unfolding.

Unfold.

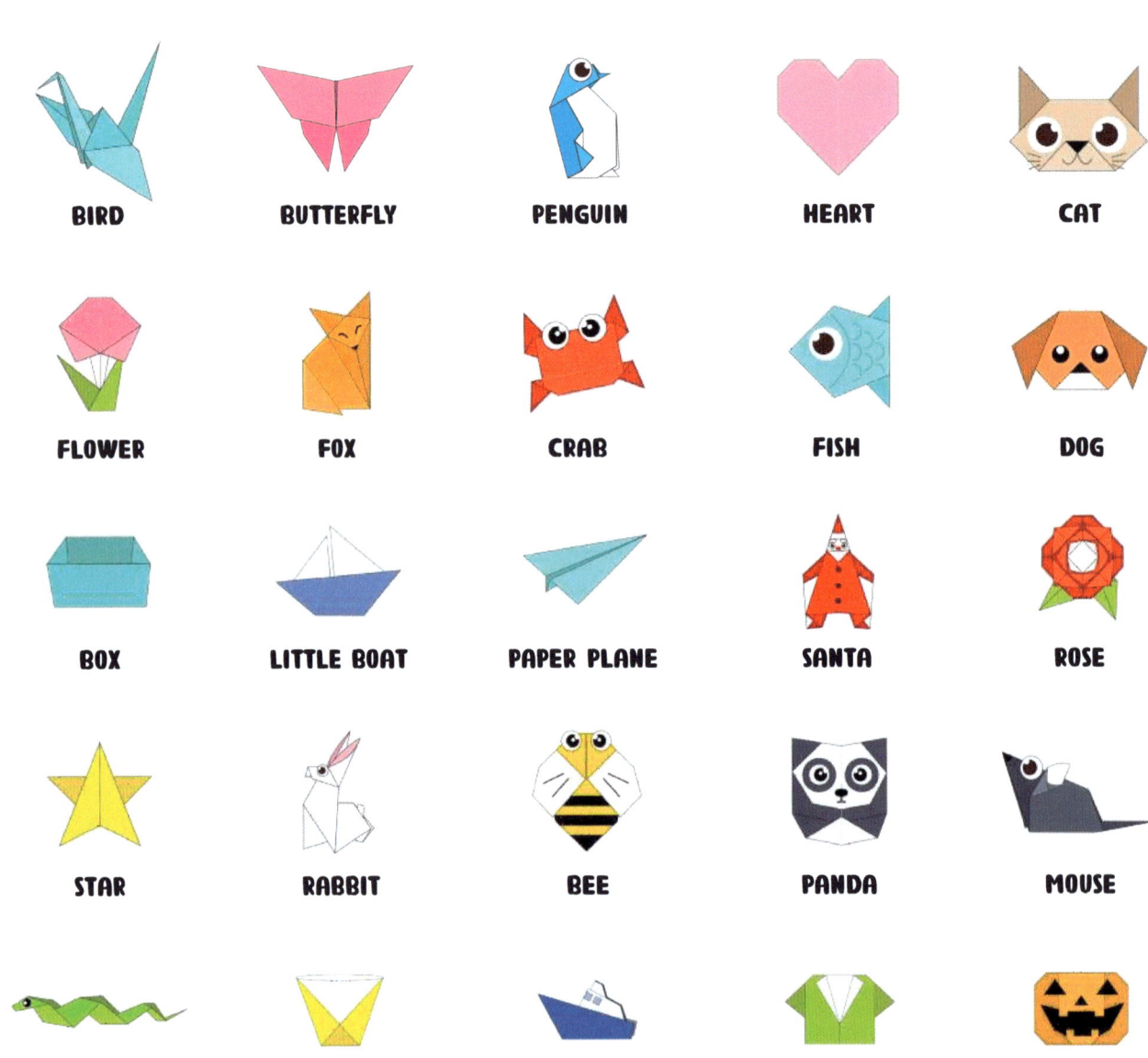

AND MUCH MORE...

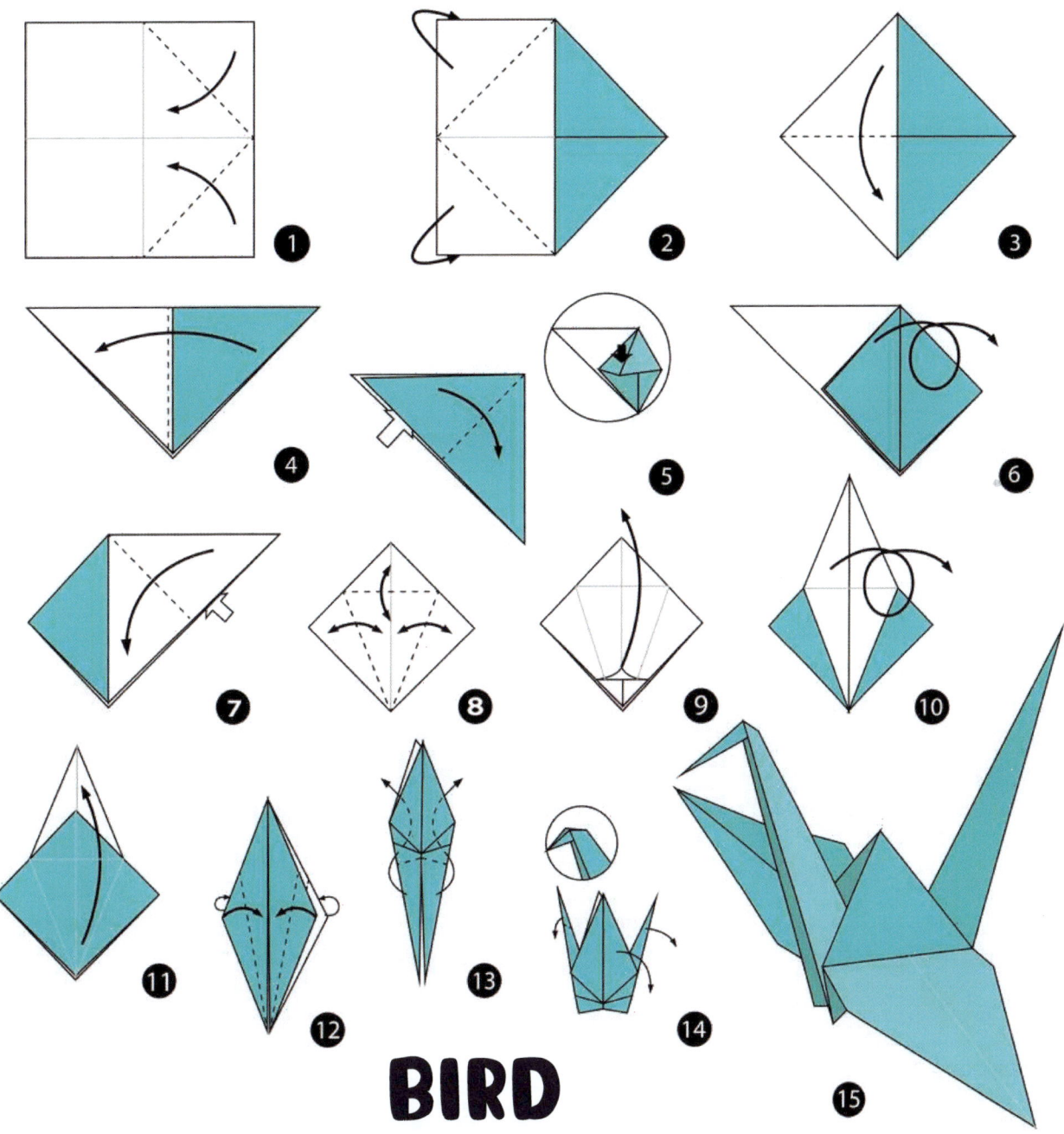

BIRD

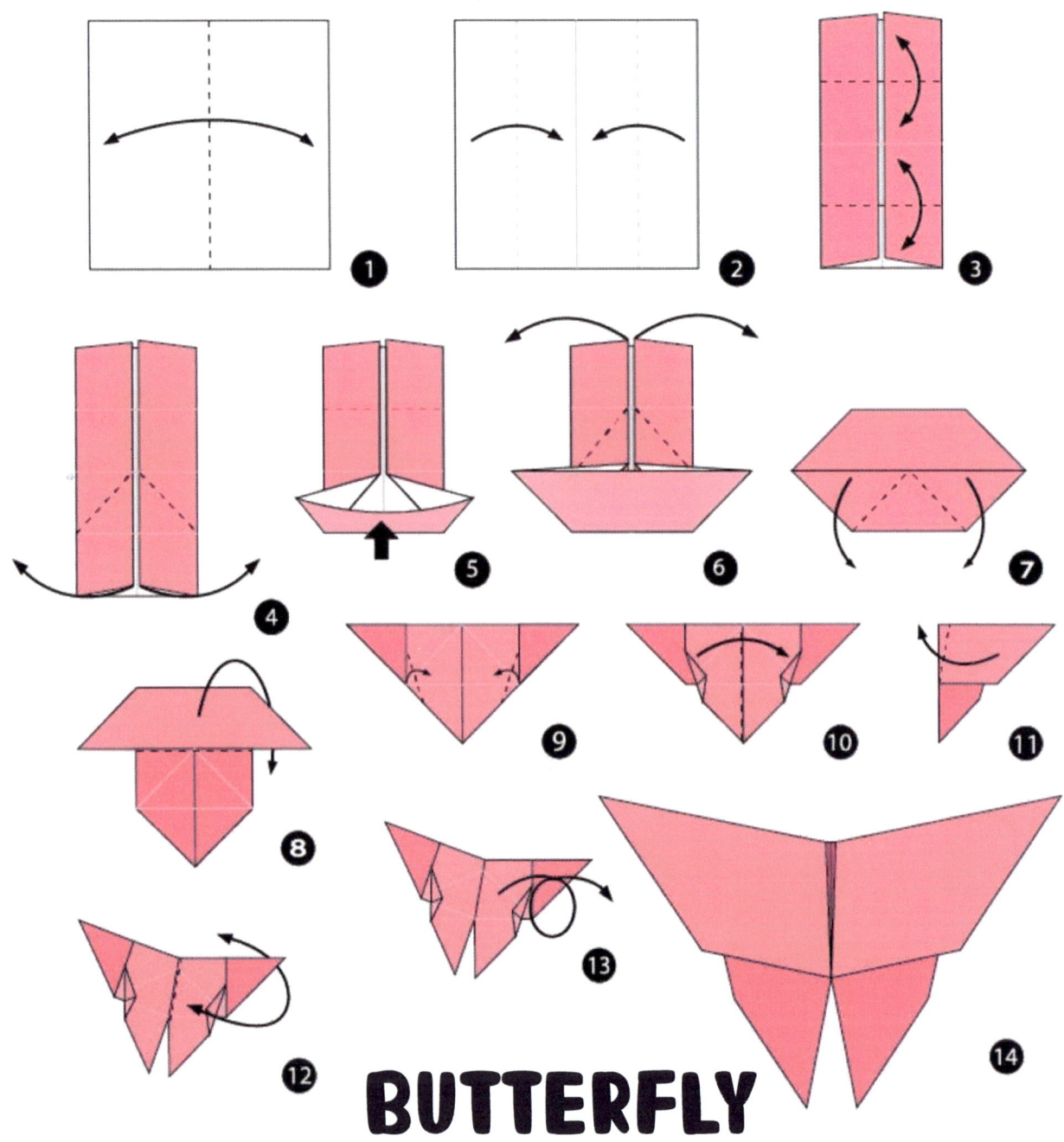

BUTTERFLY

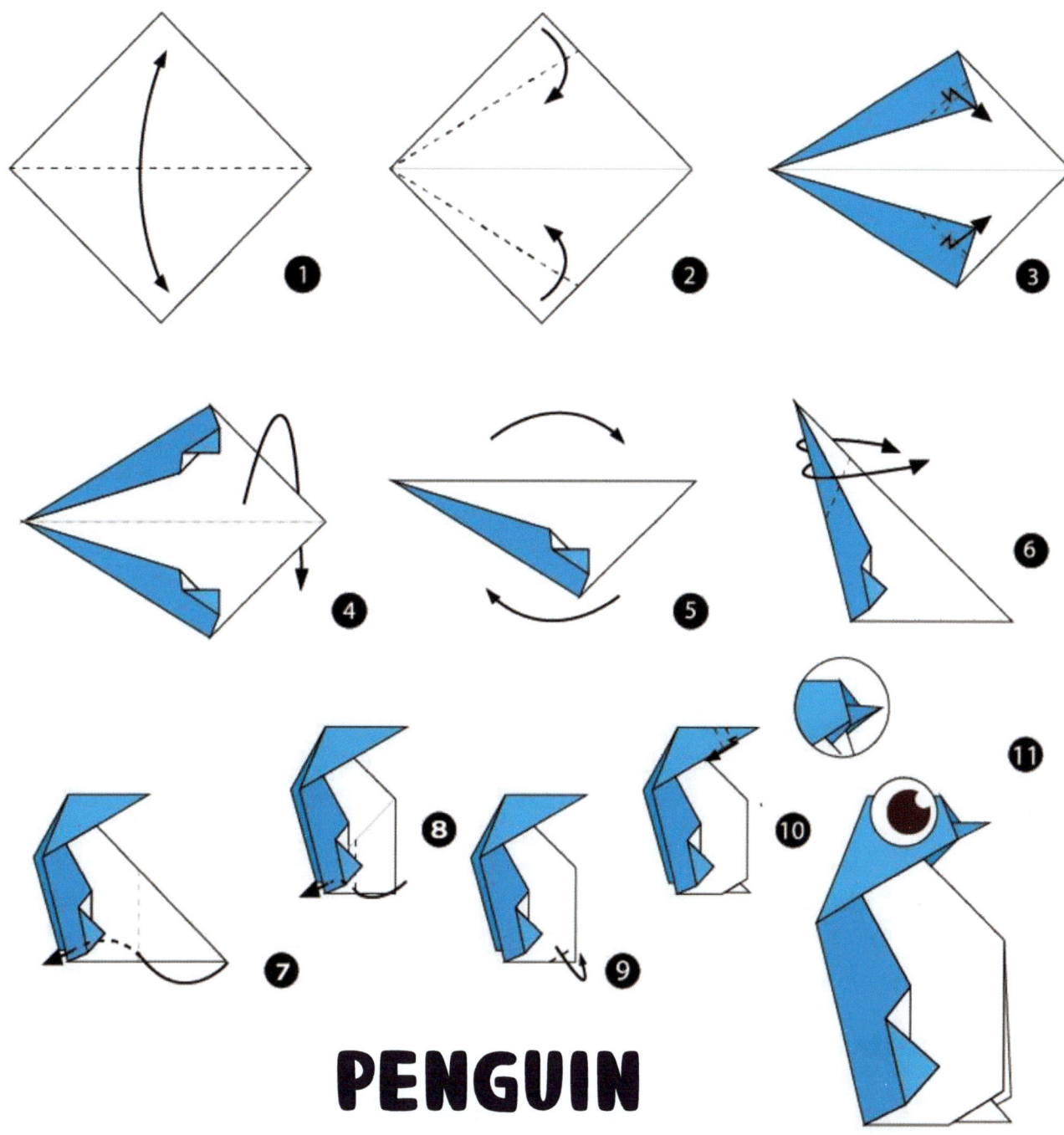

PENGUIN

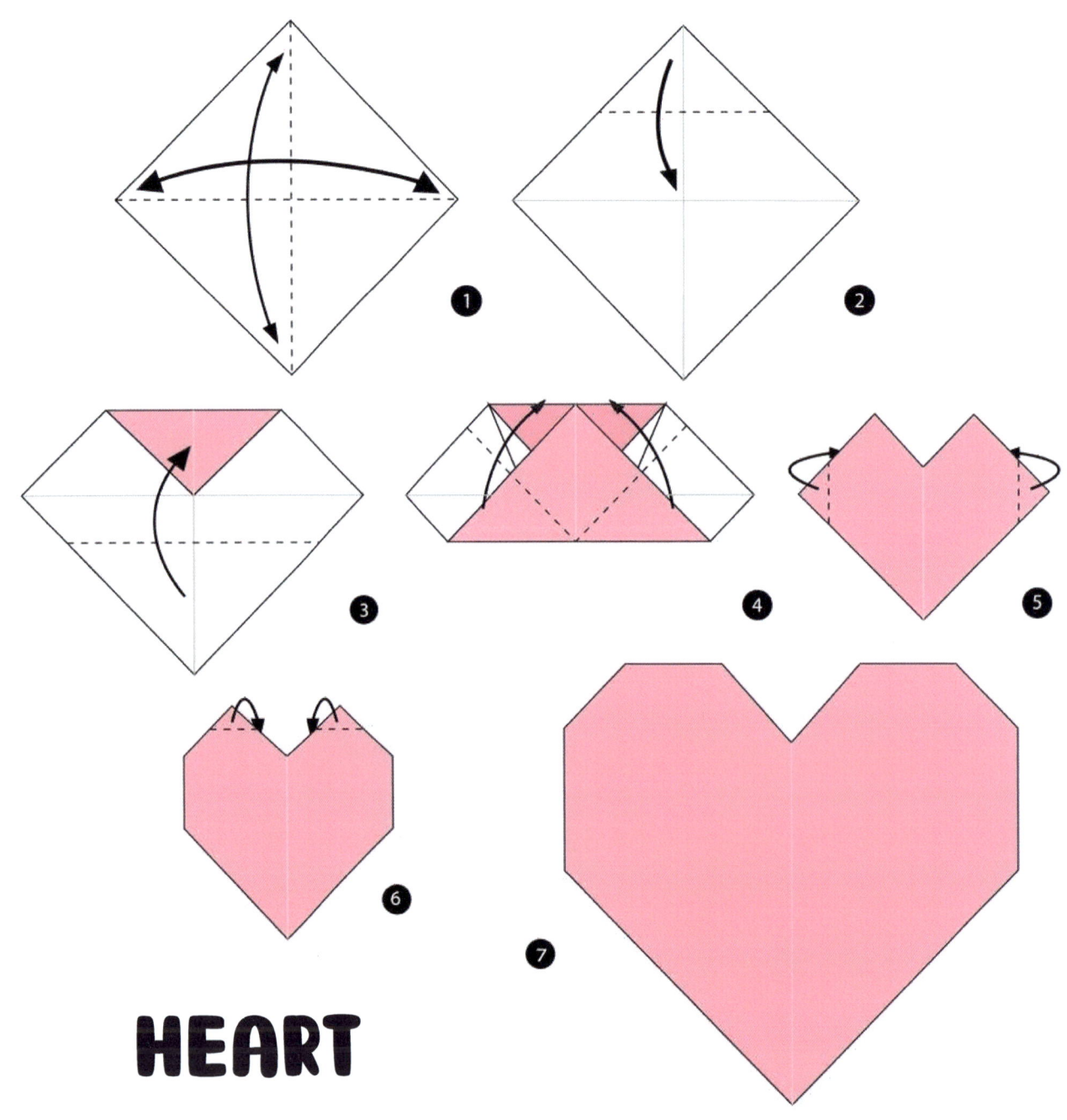

HEART

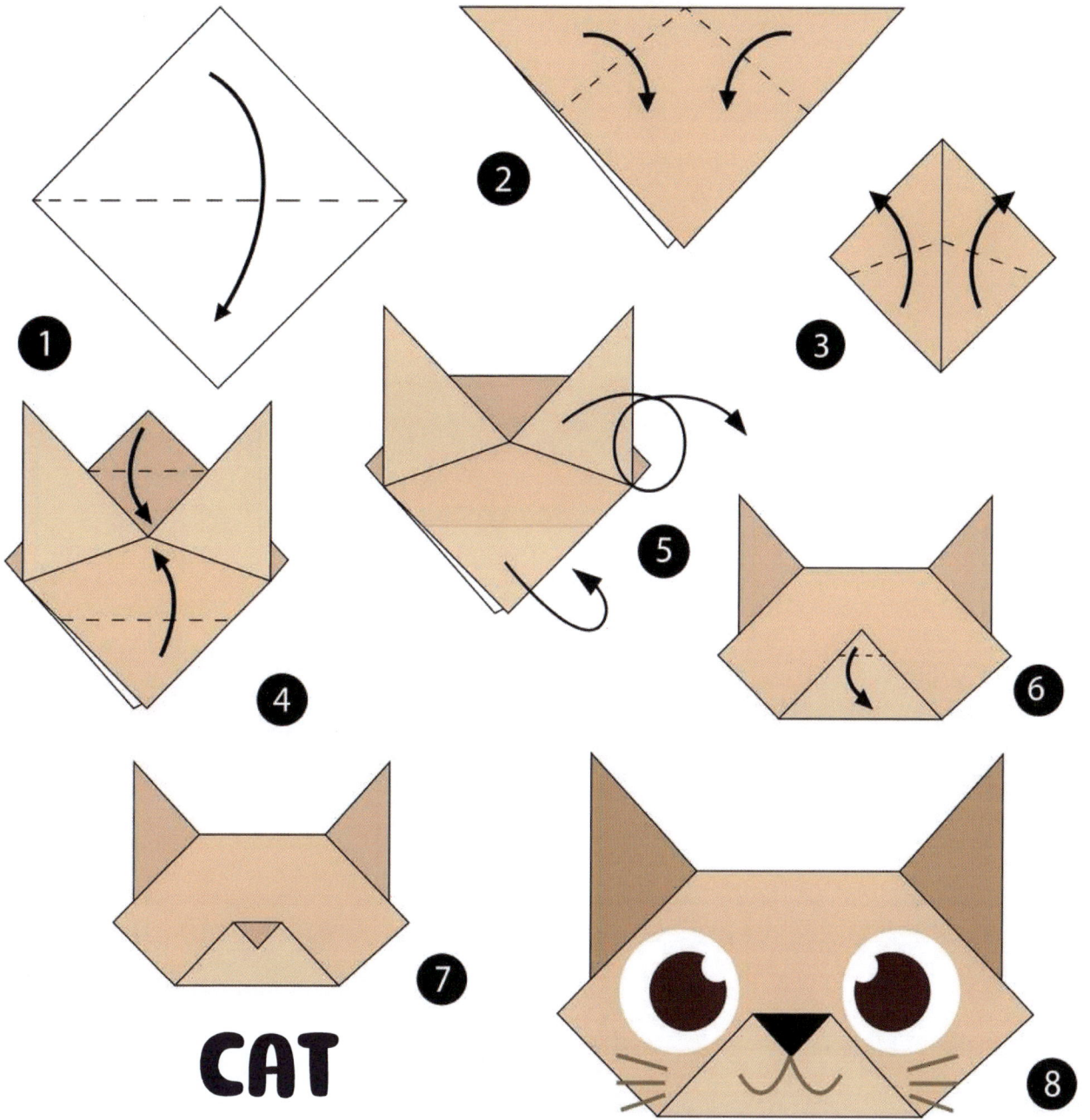

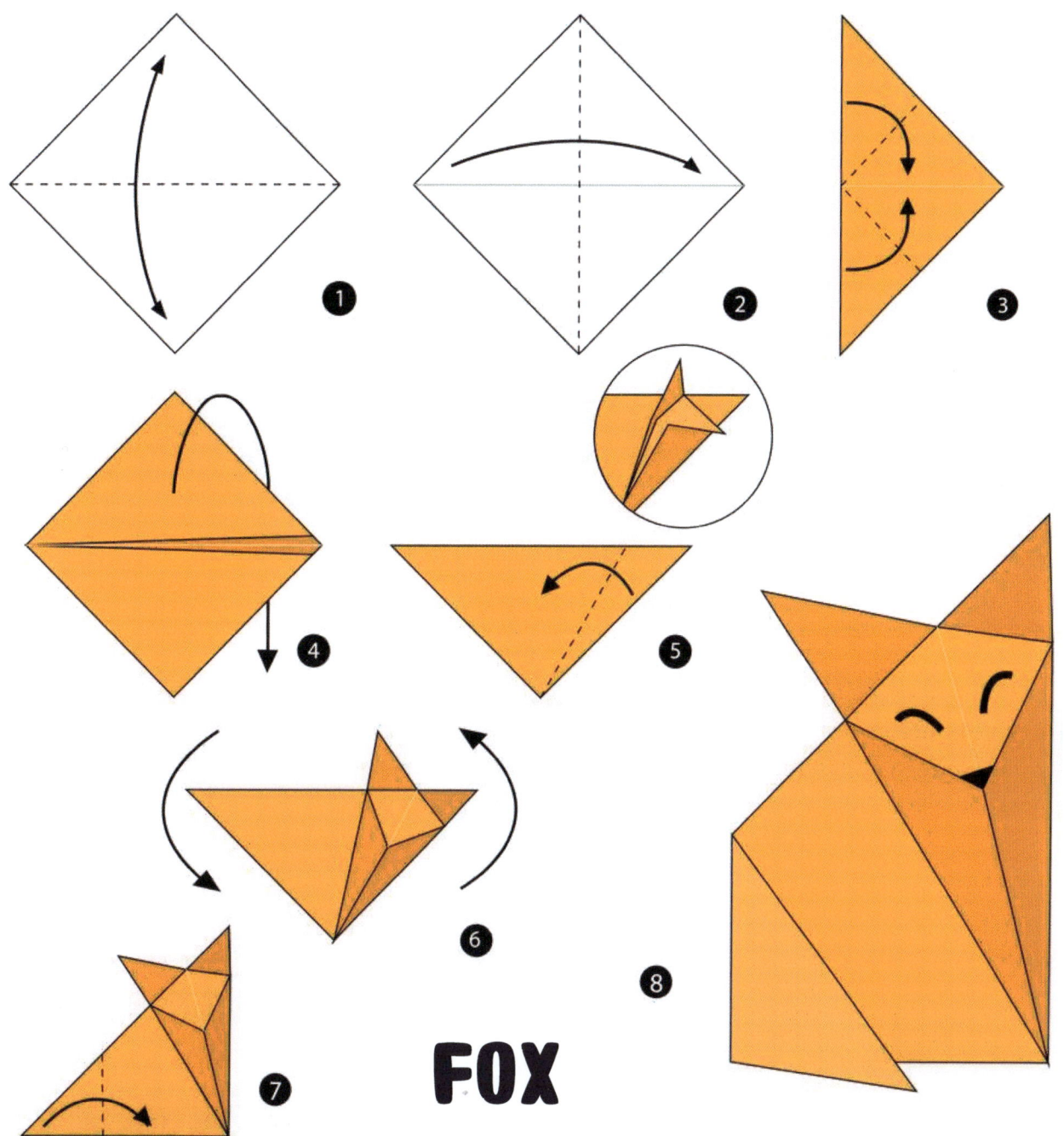

FOX

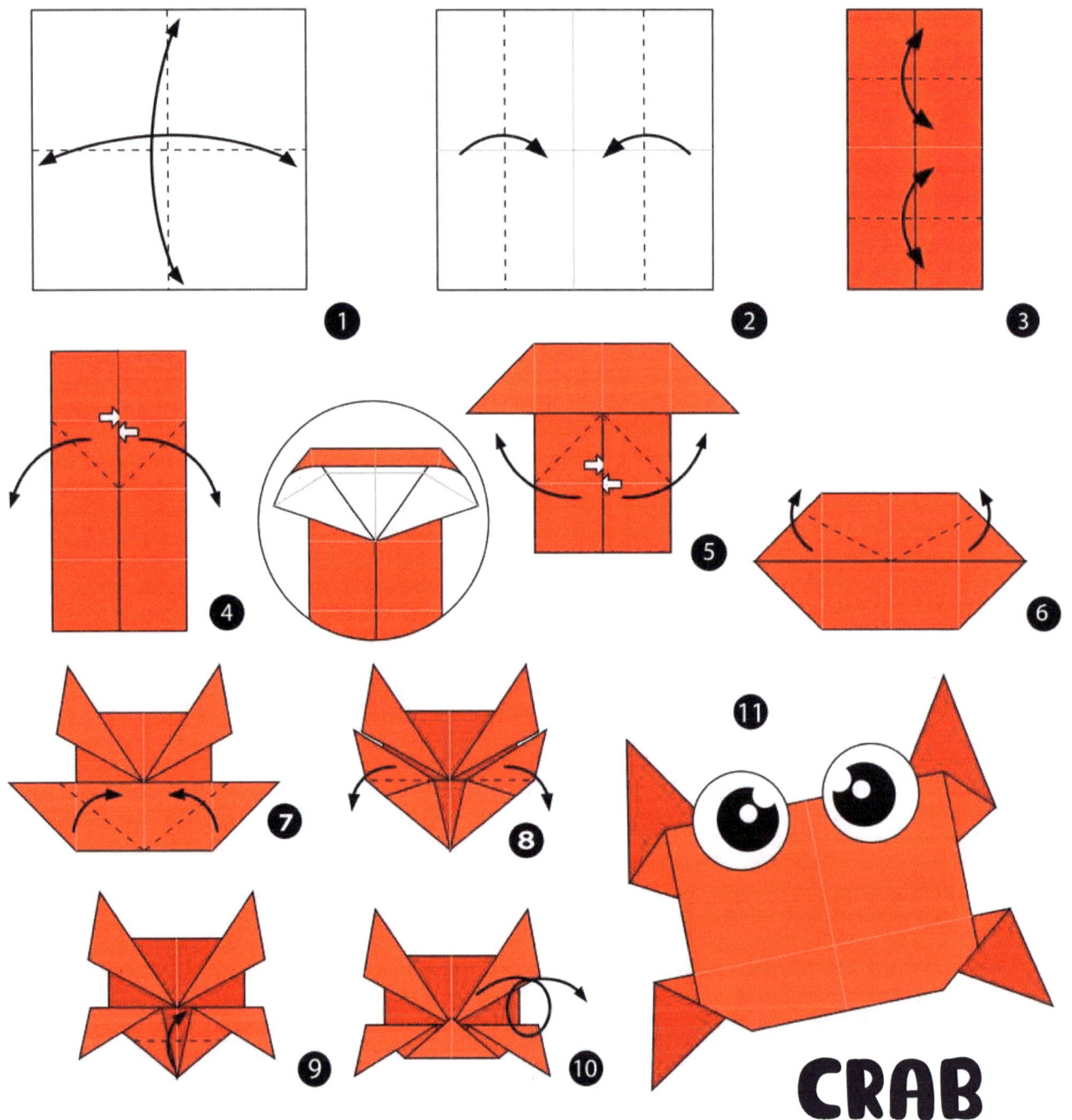

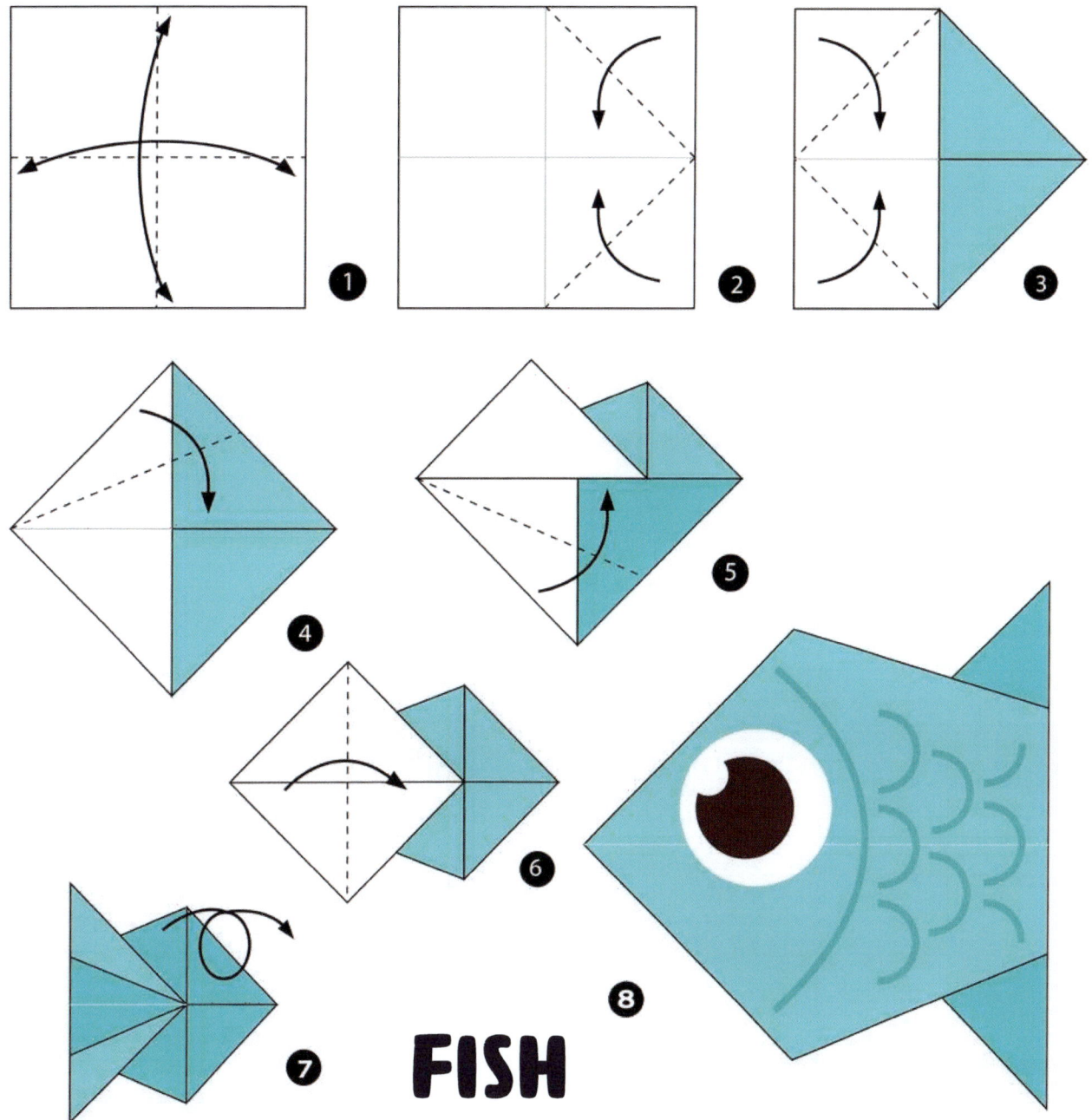

FISH

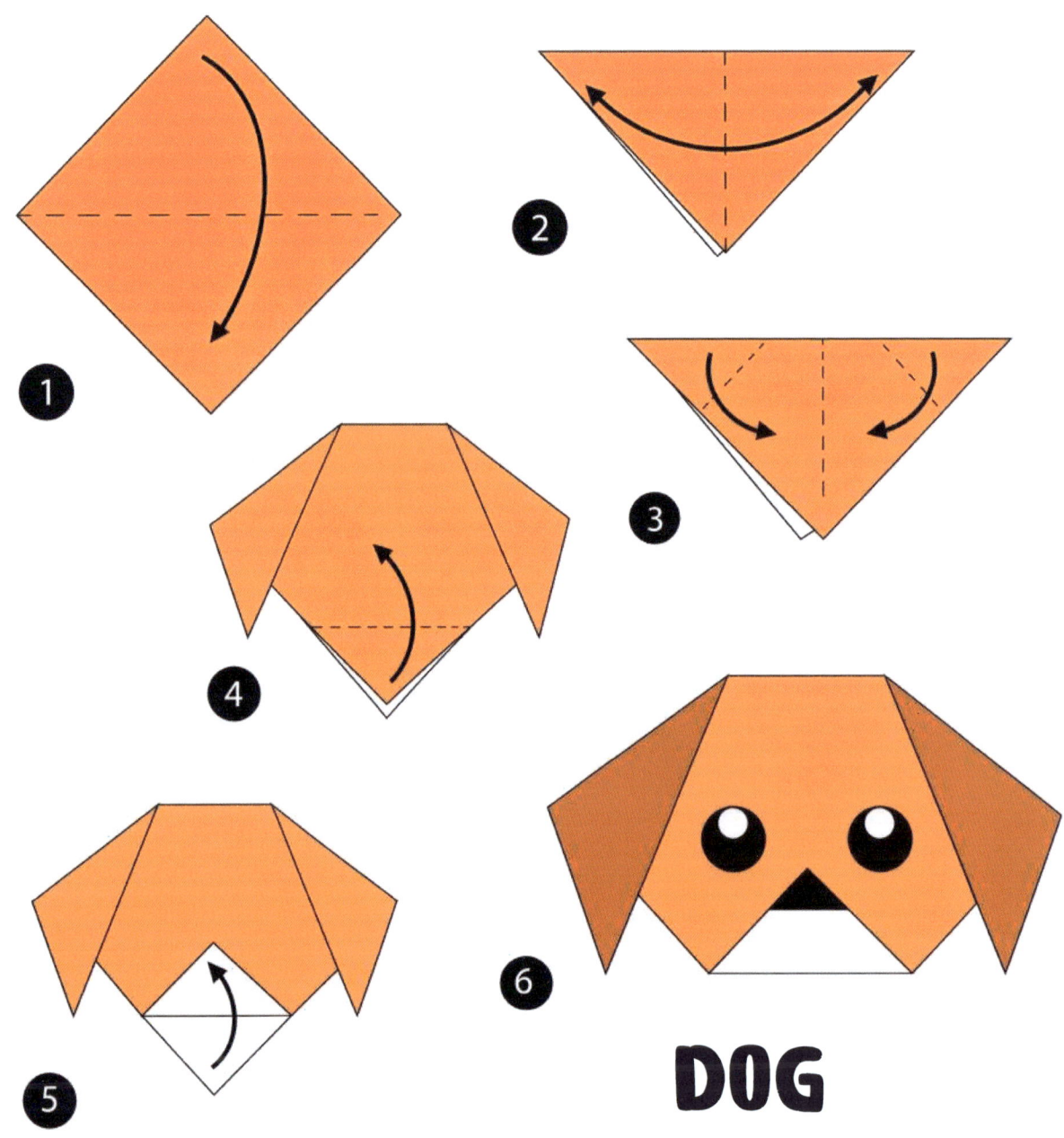

DOG

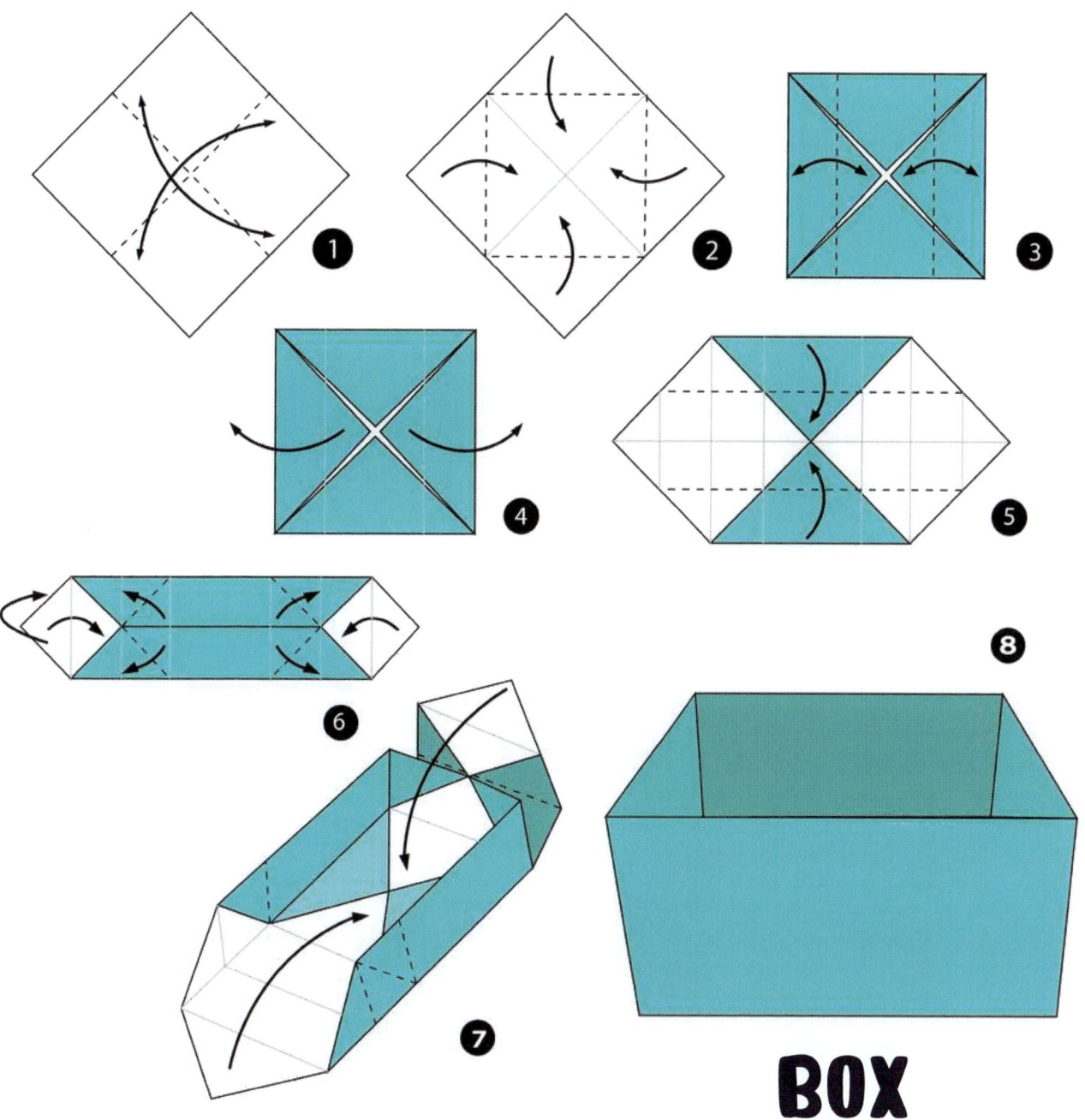

BOX

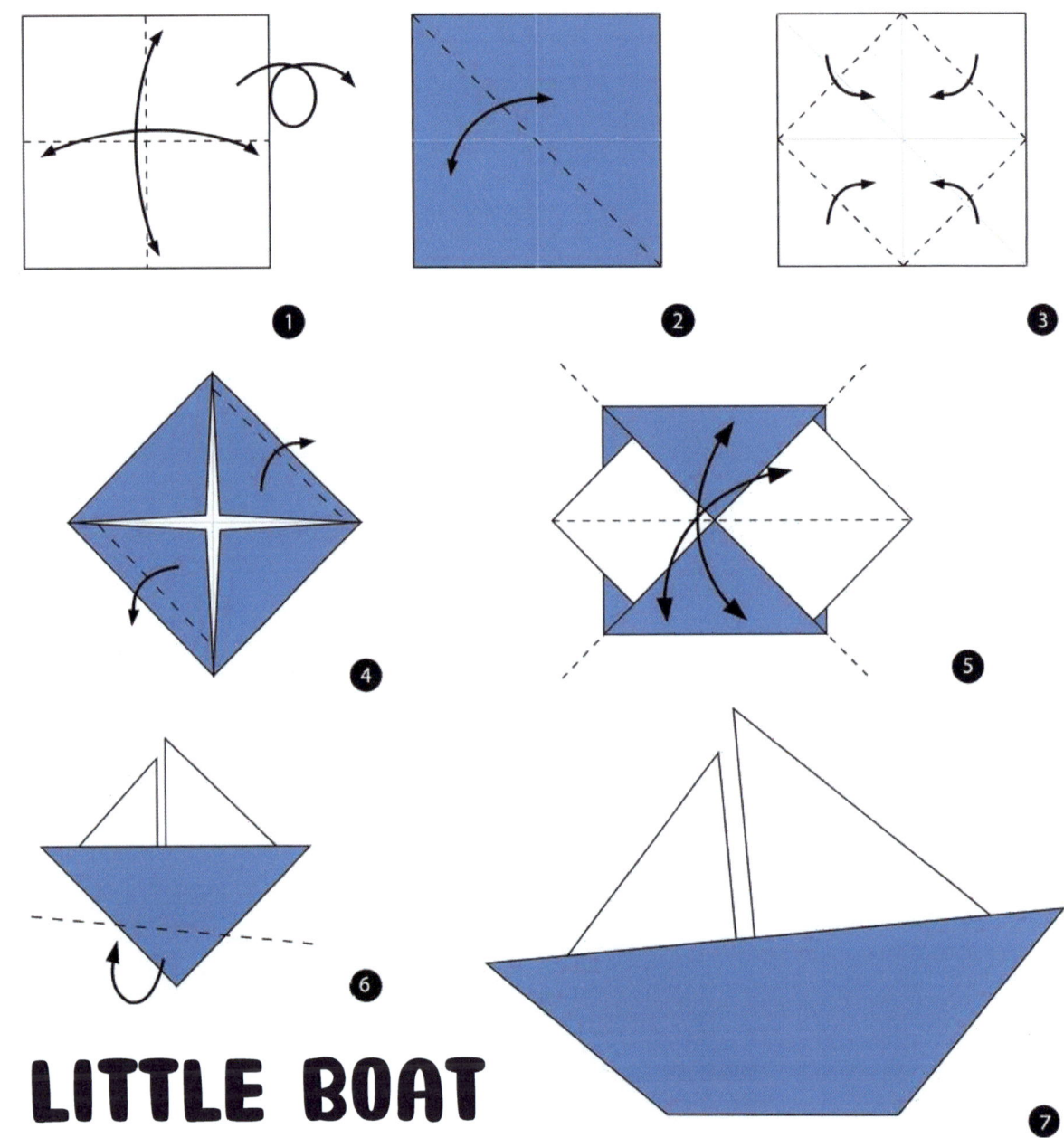

LITTLE BOAT

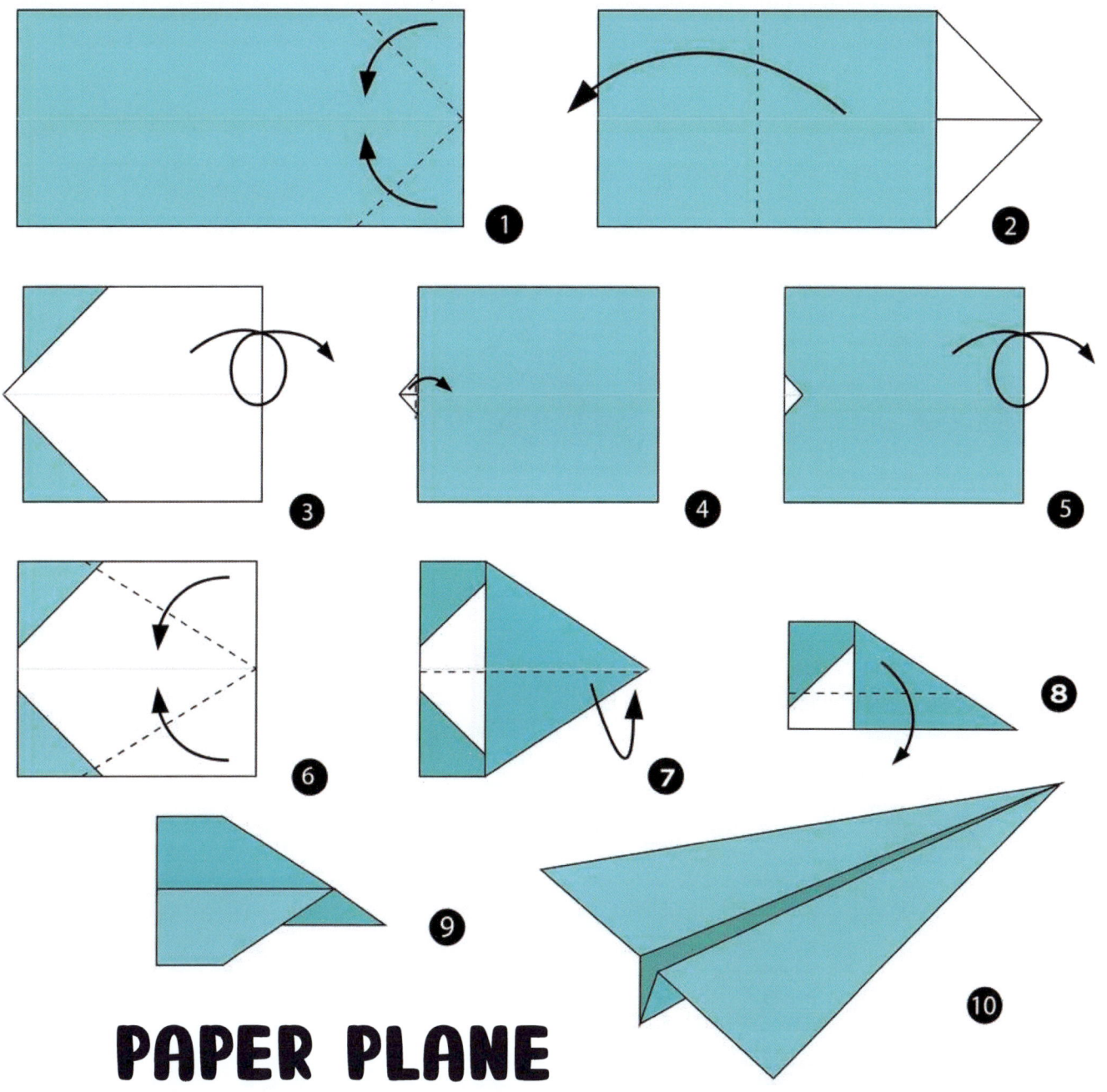

PAPER PLANE

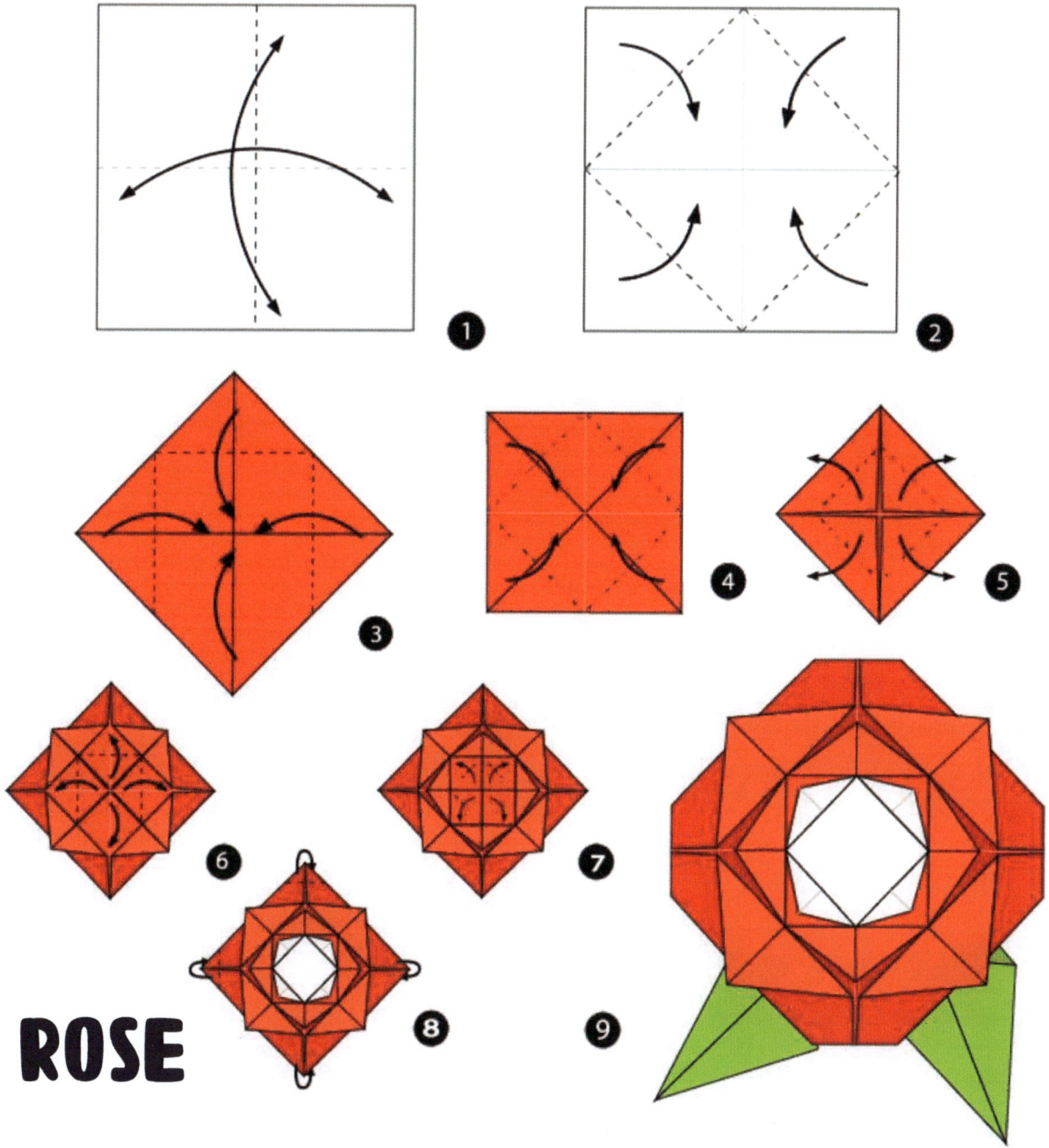

ROSE

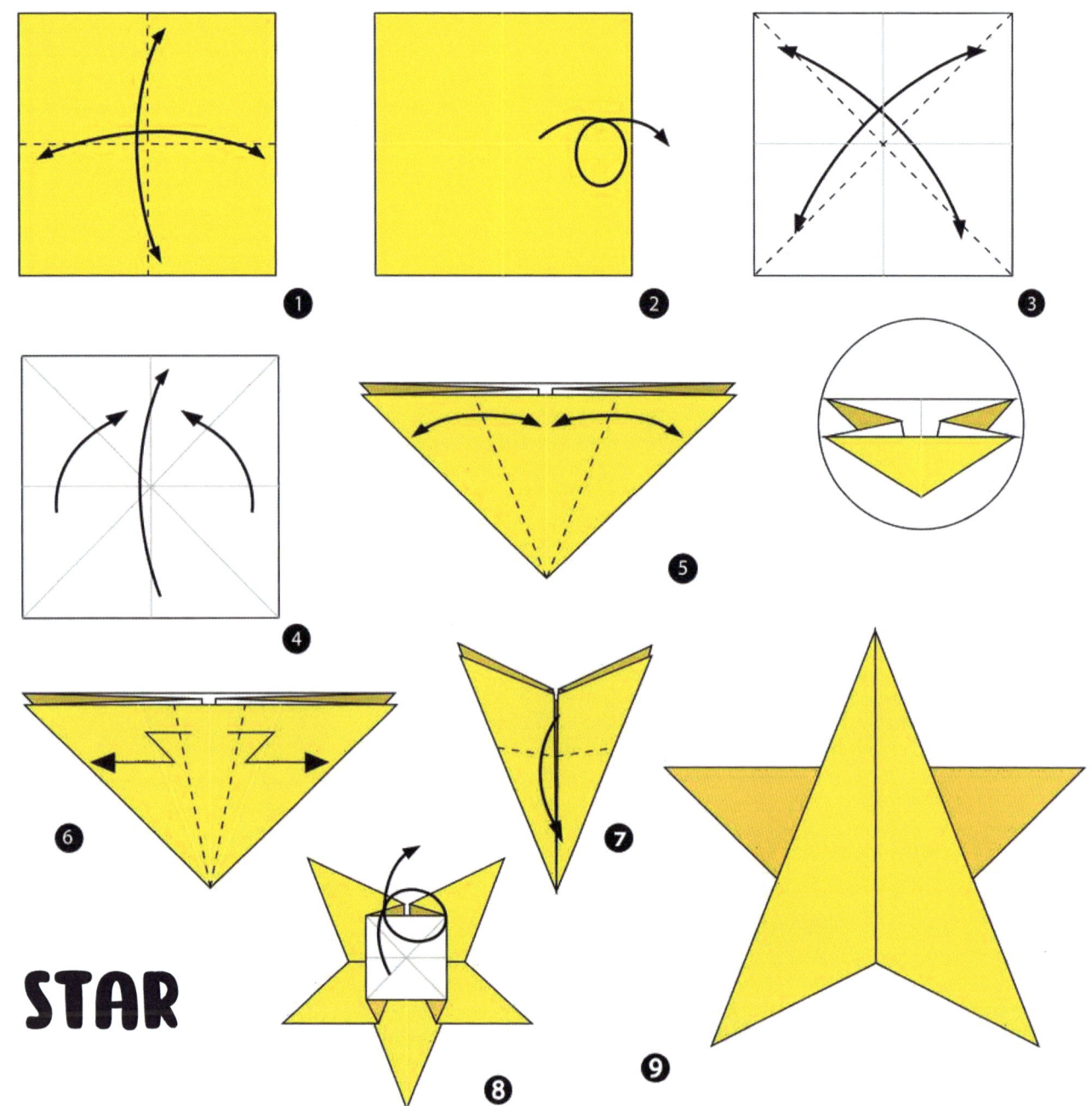

STAR

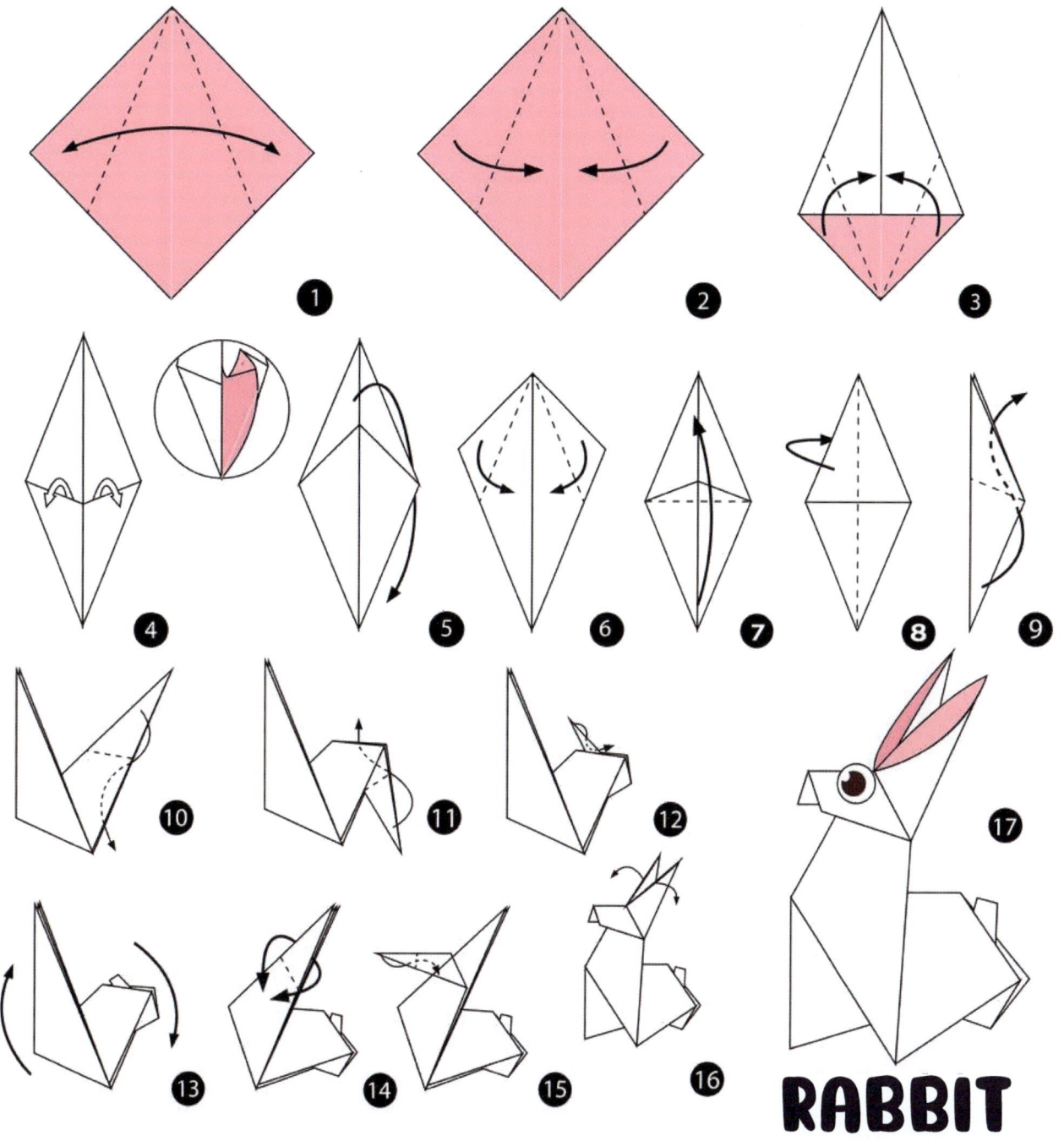

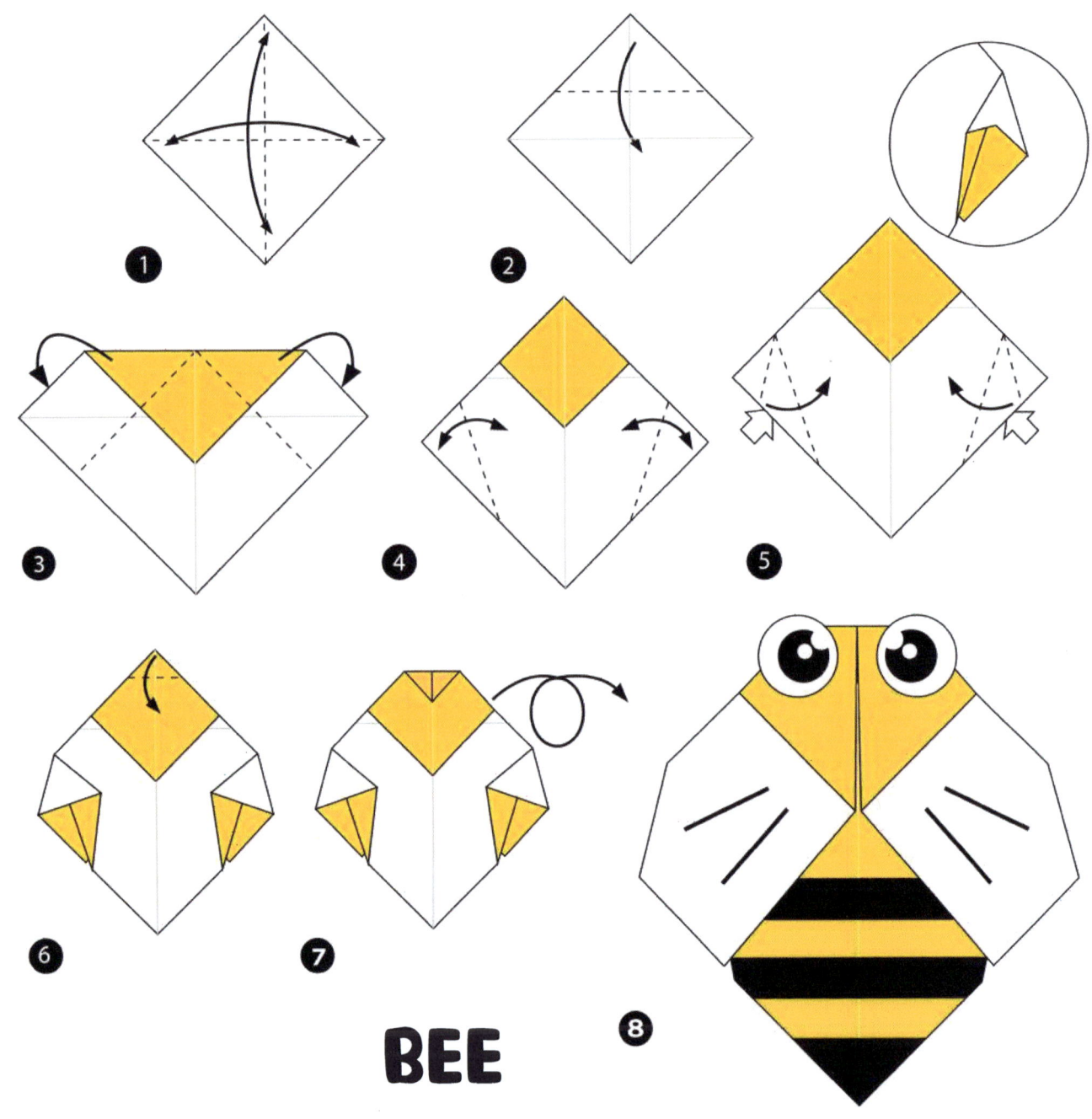

BEE

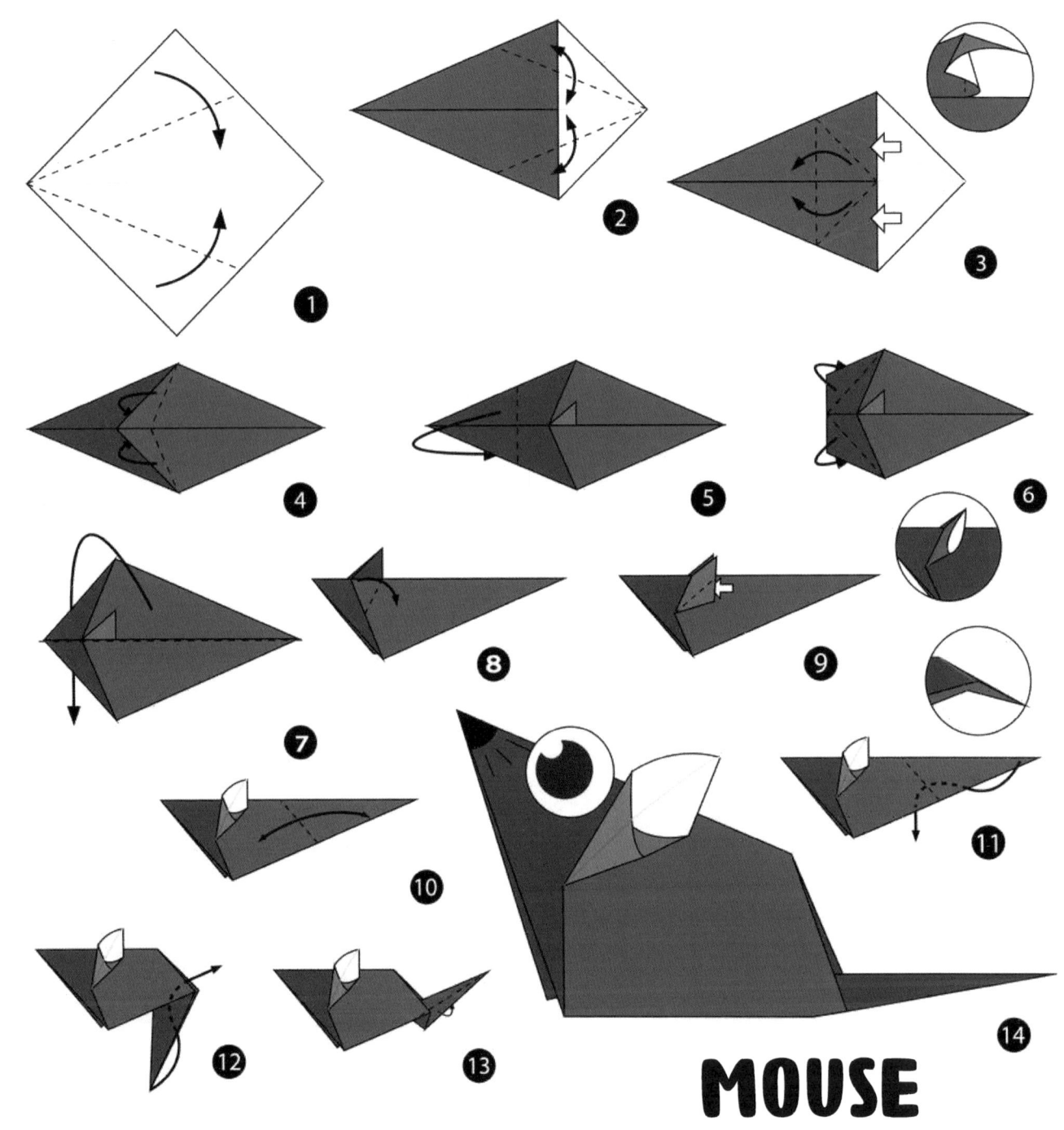

MOUSE

SNAKE

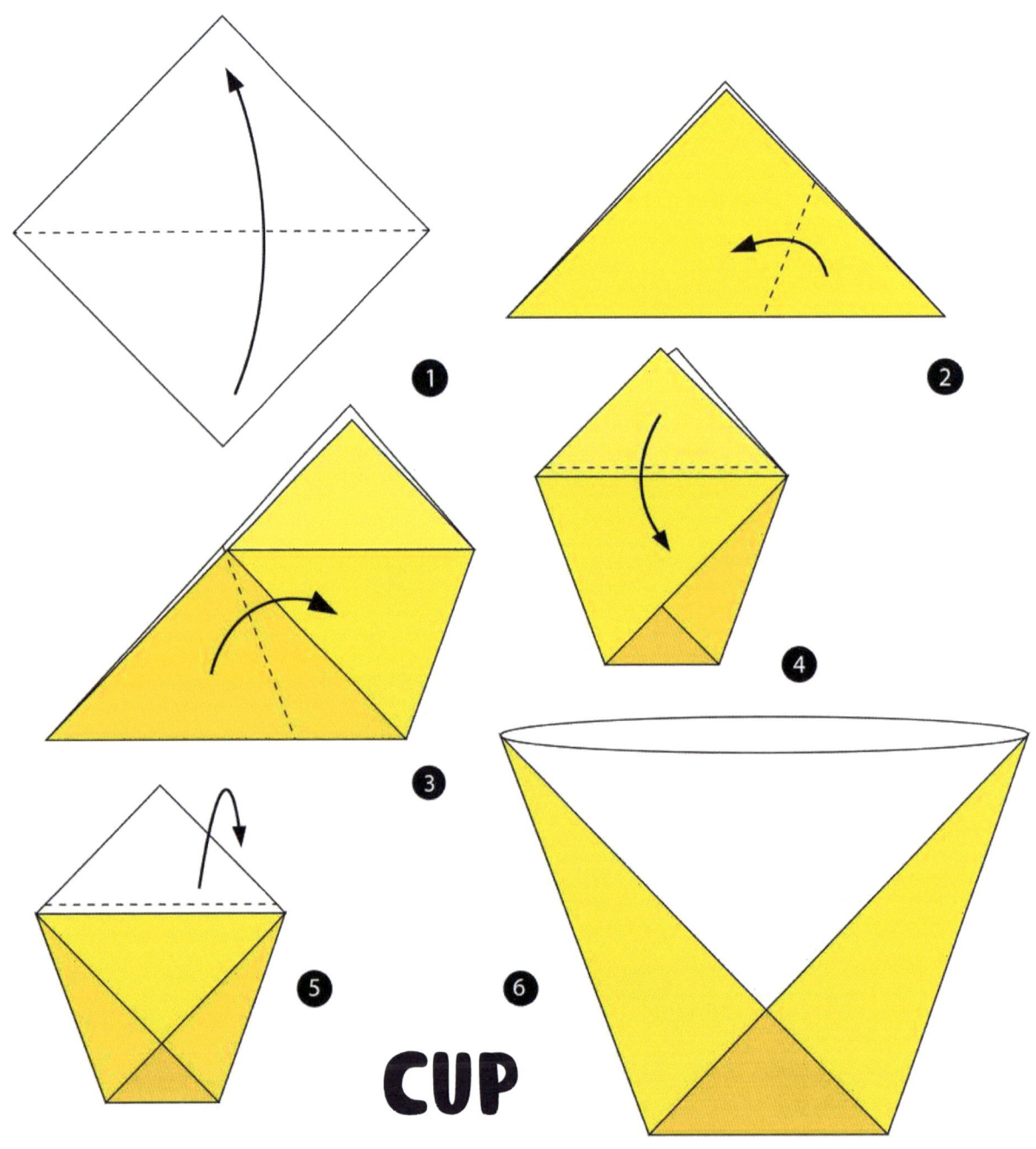

CUP

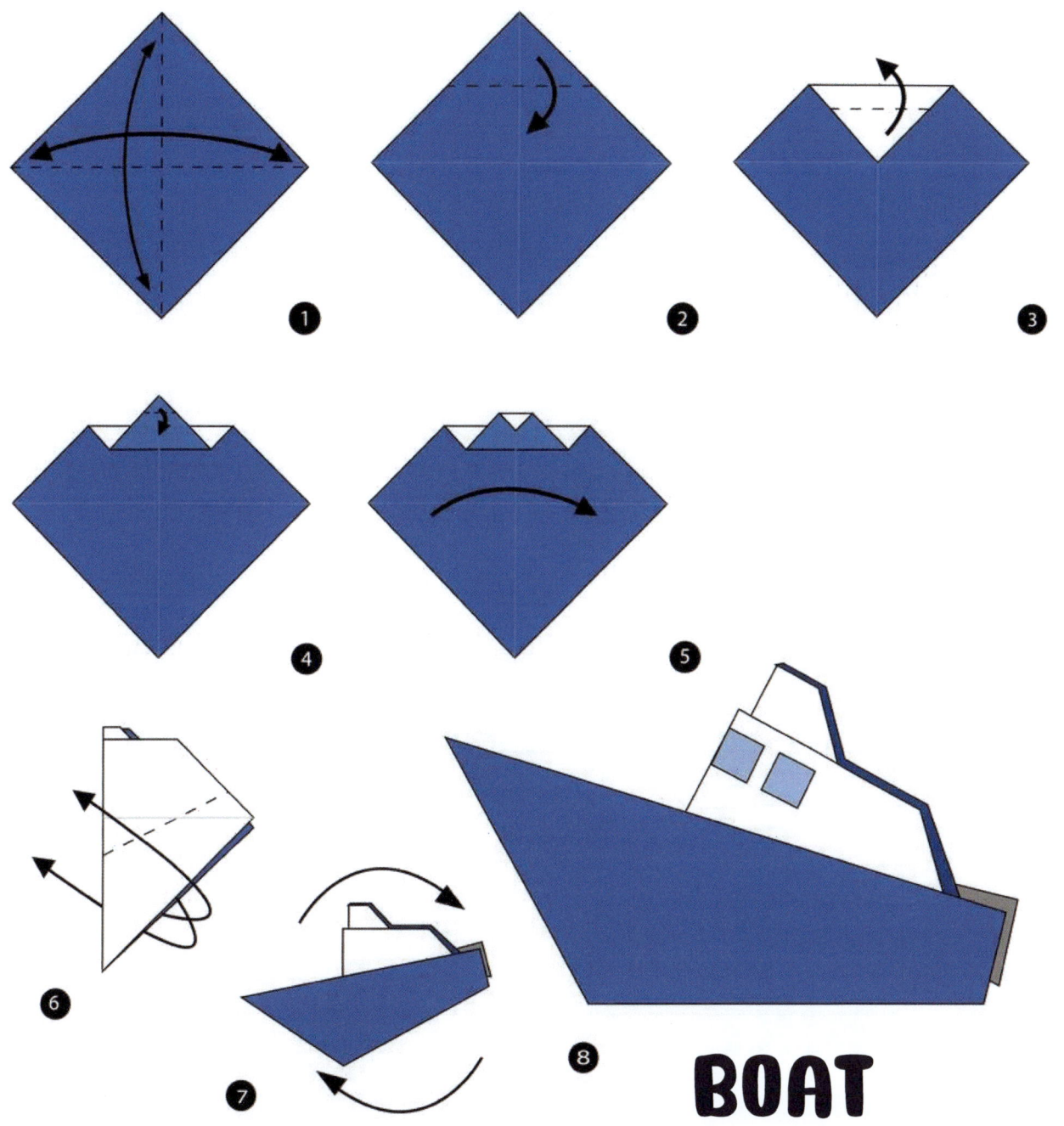

BOAT

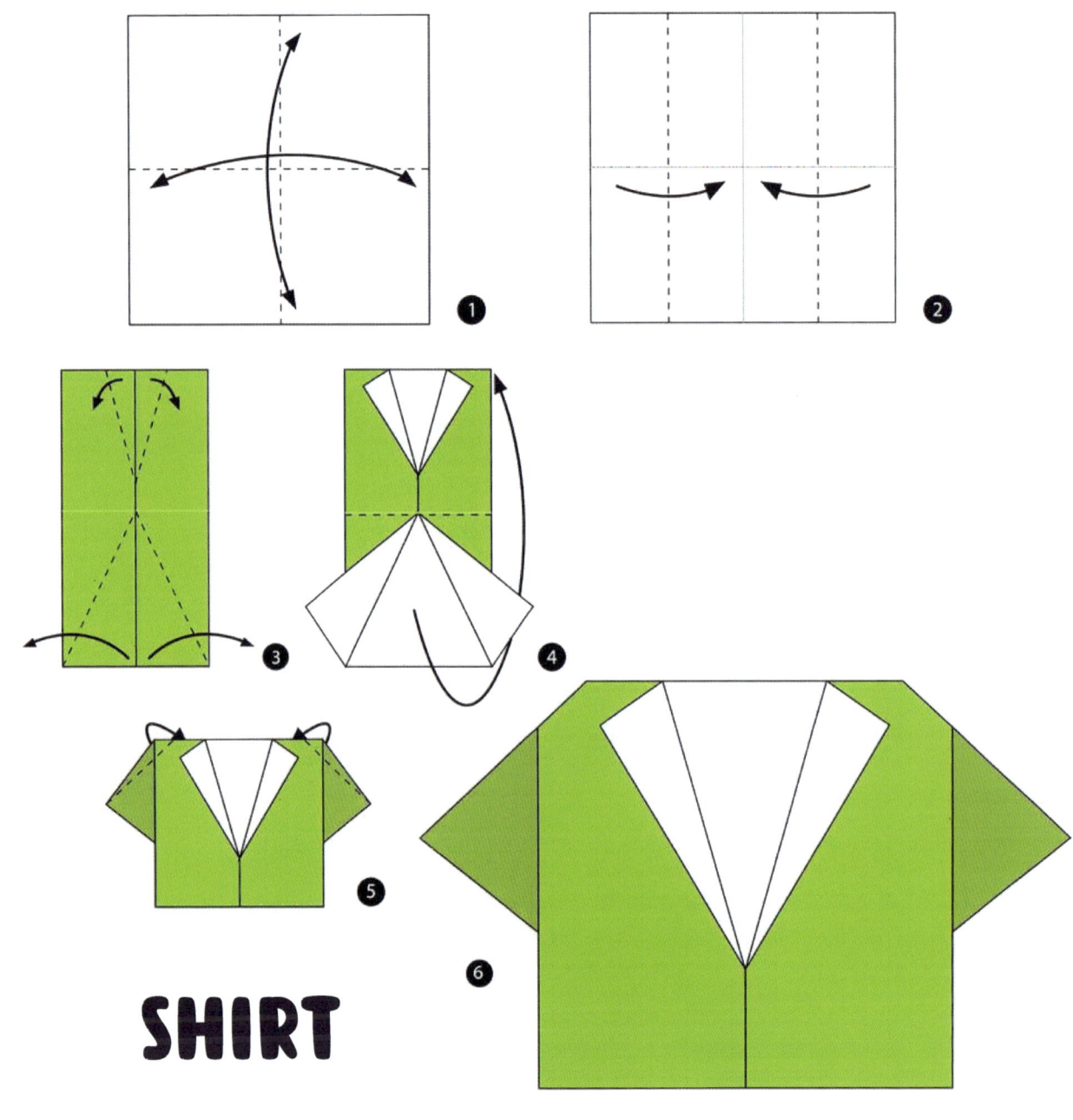

SHIRT

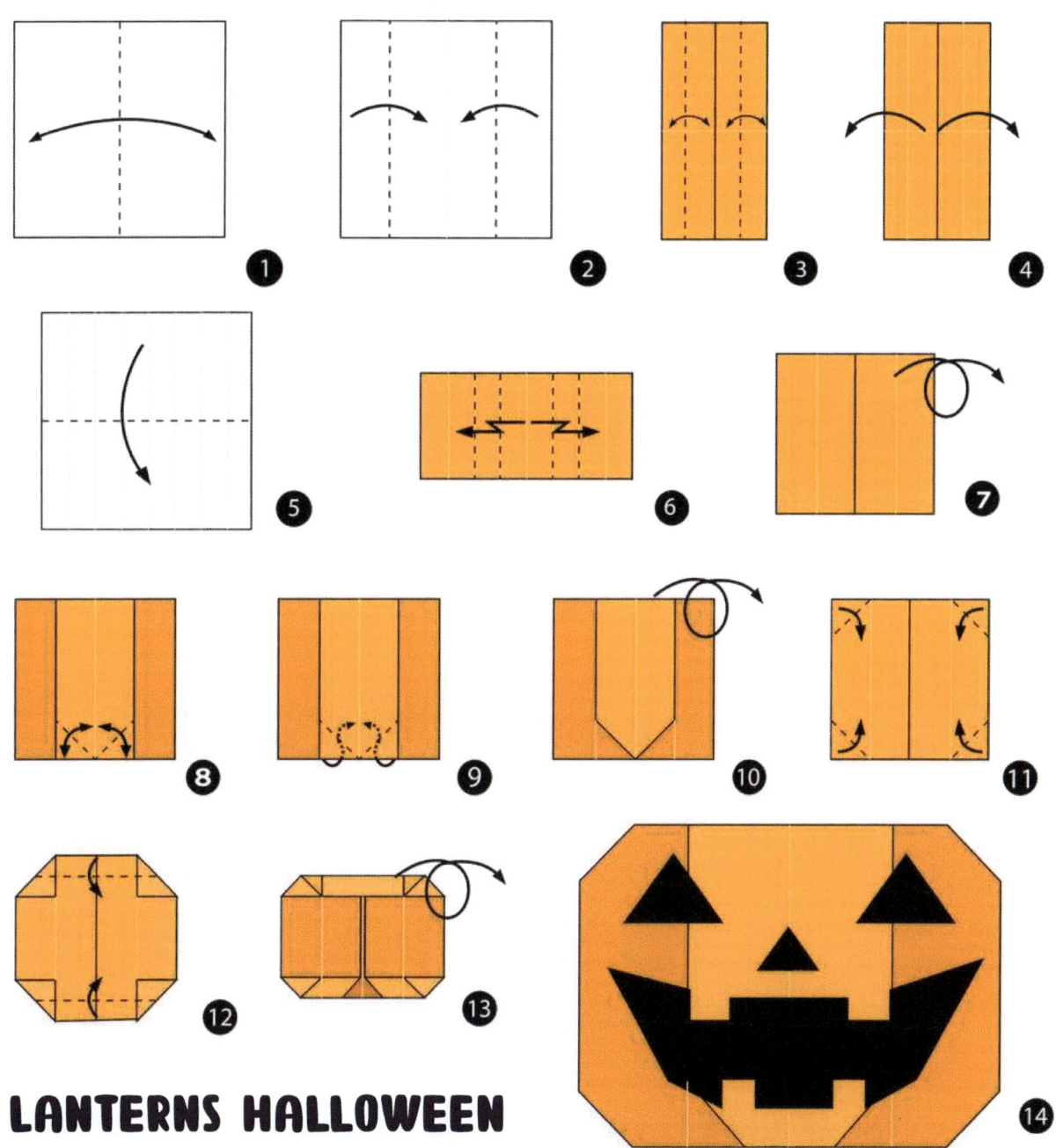

LANTERNS HALLOWEEN

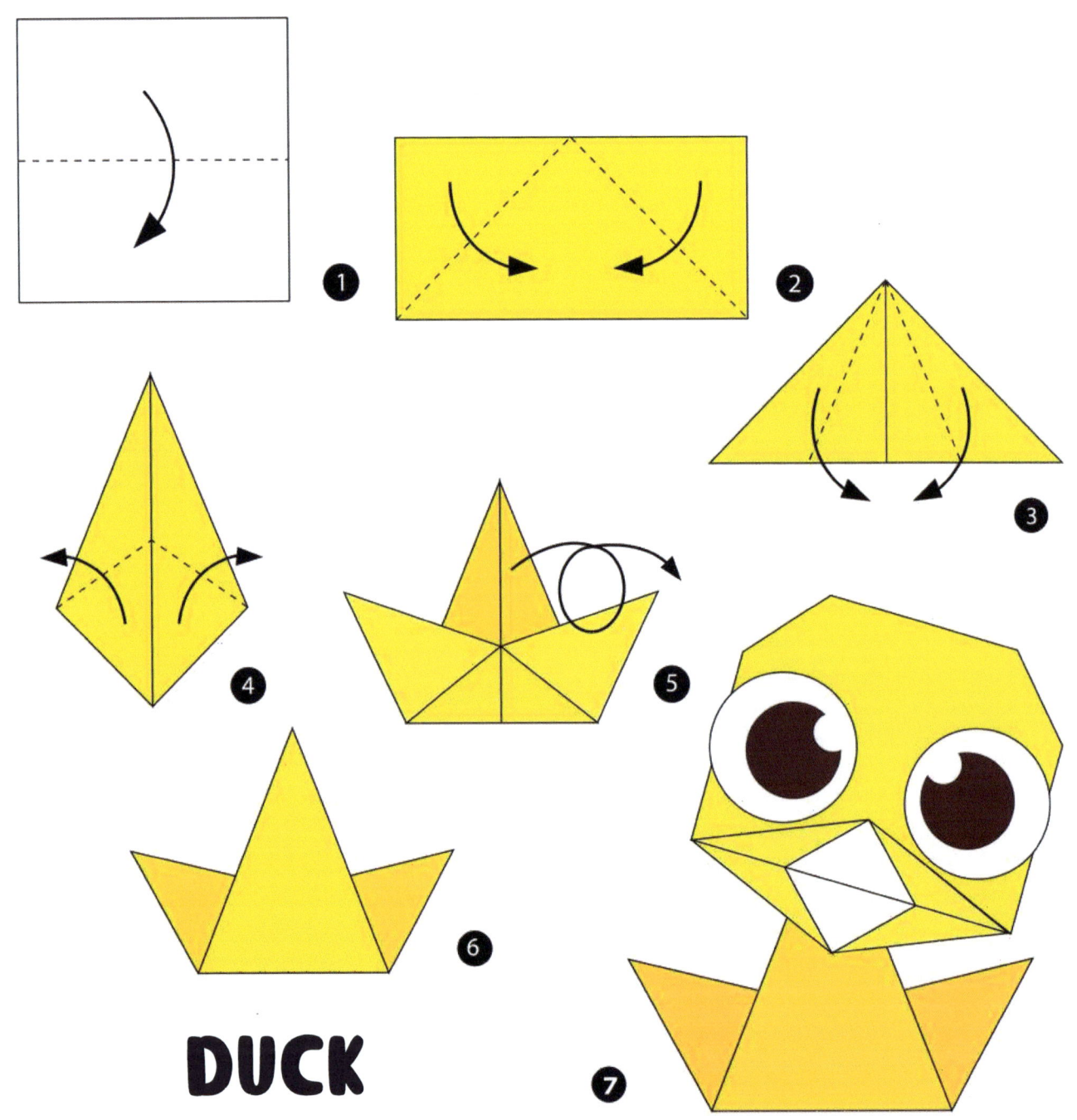

DUCK

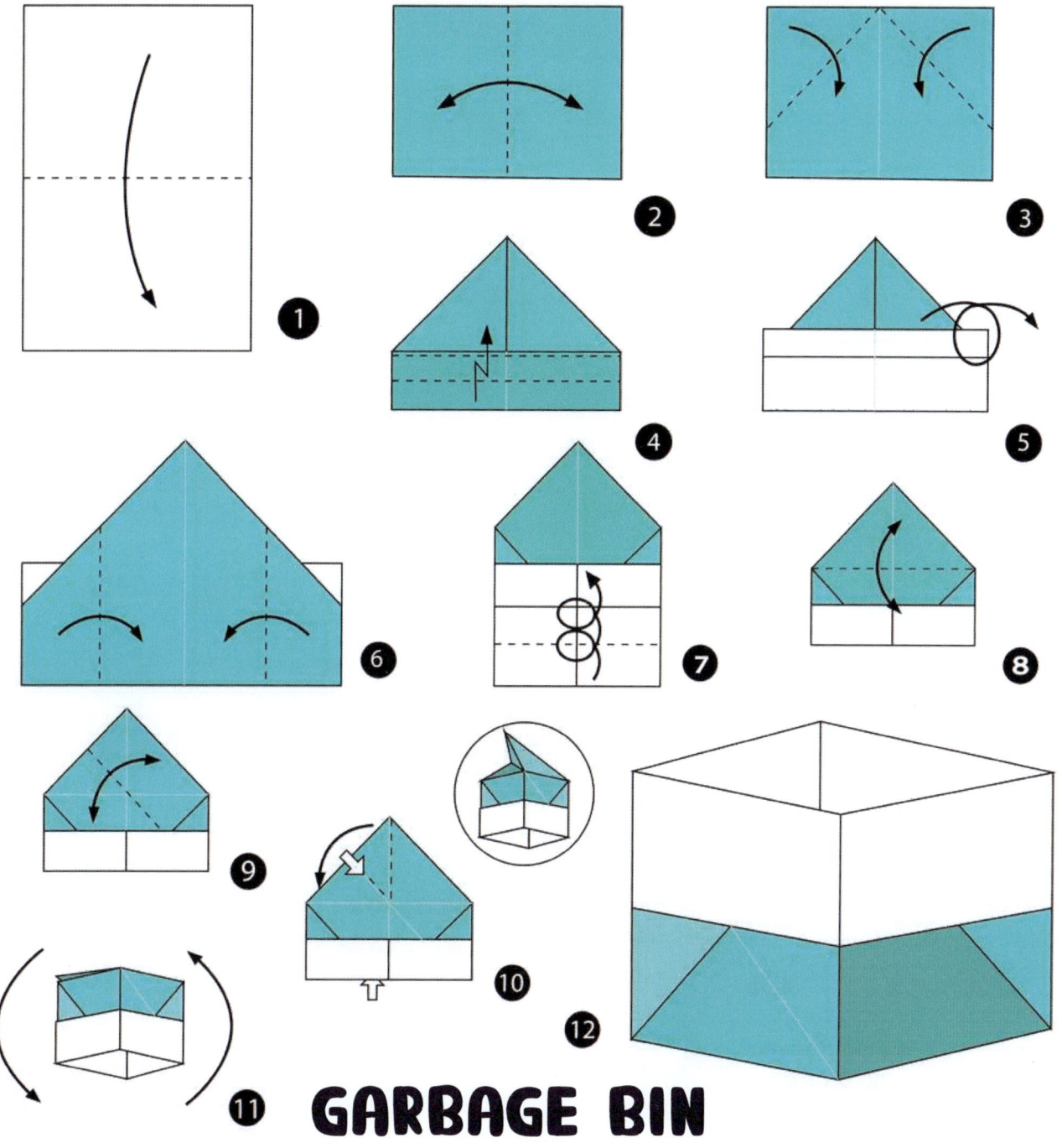

GARBAGE BIN

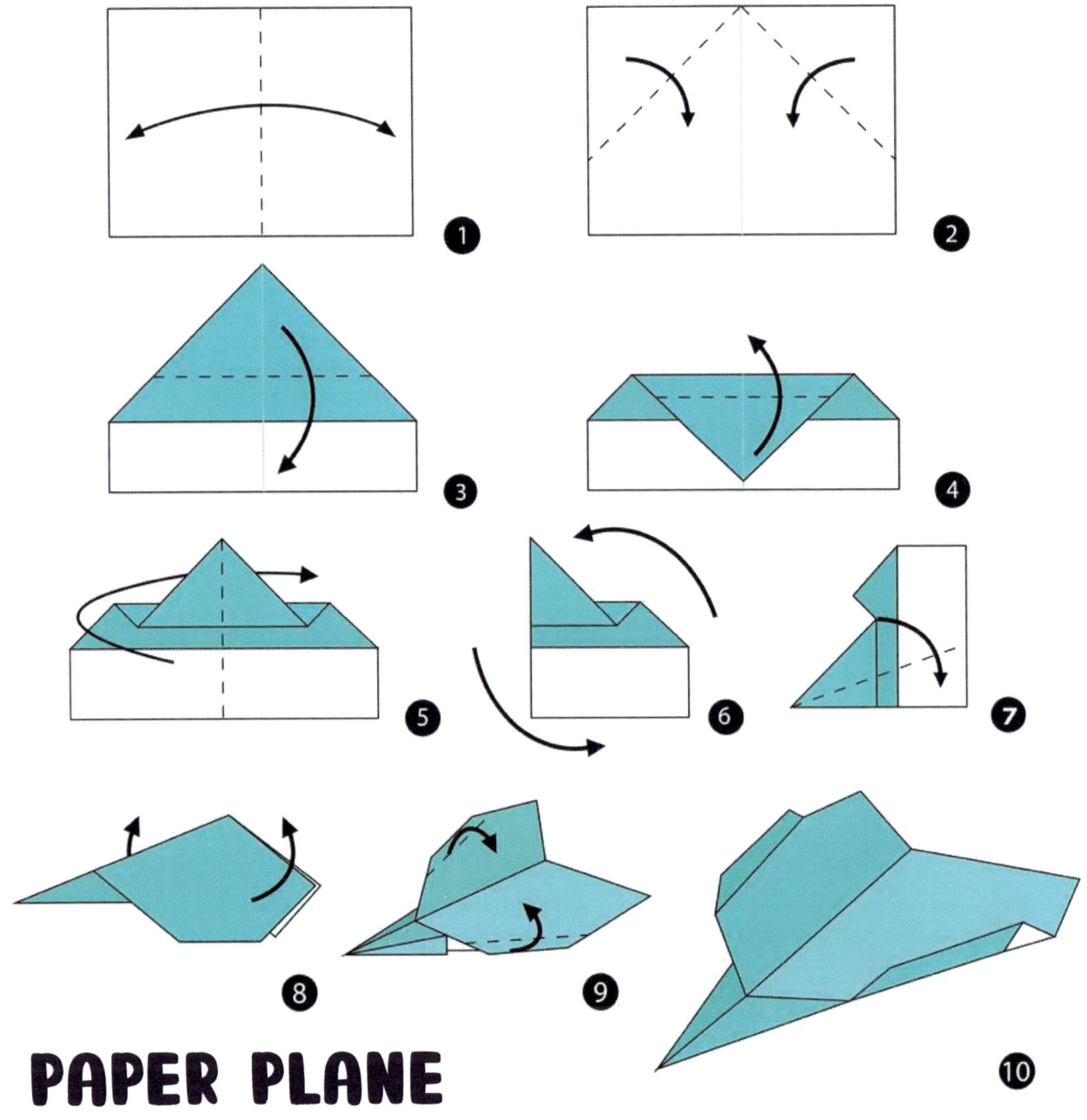

PAPER PLANE

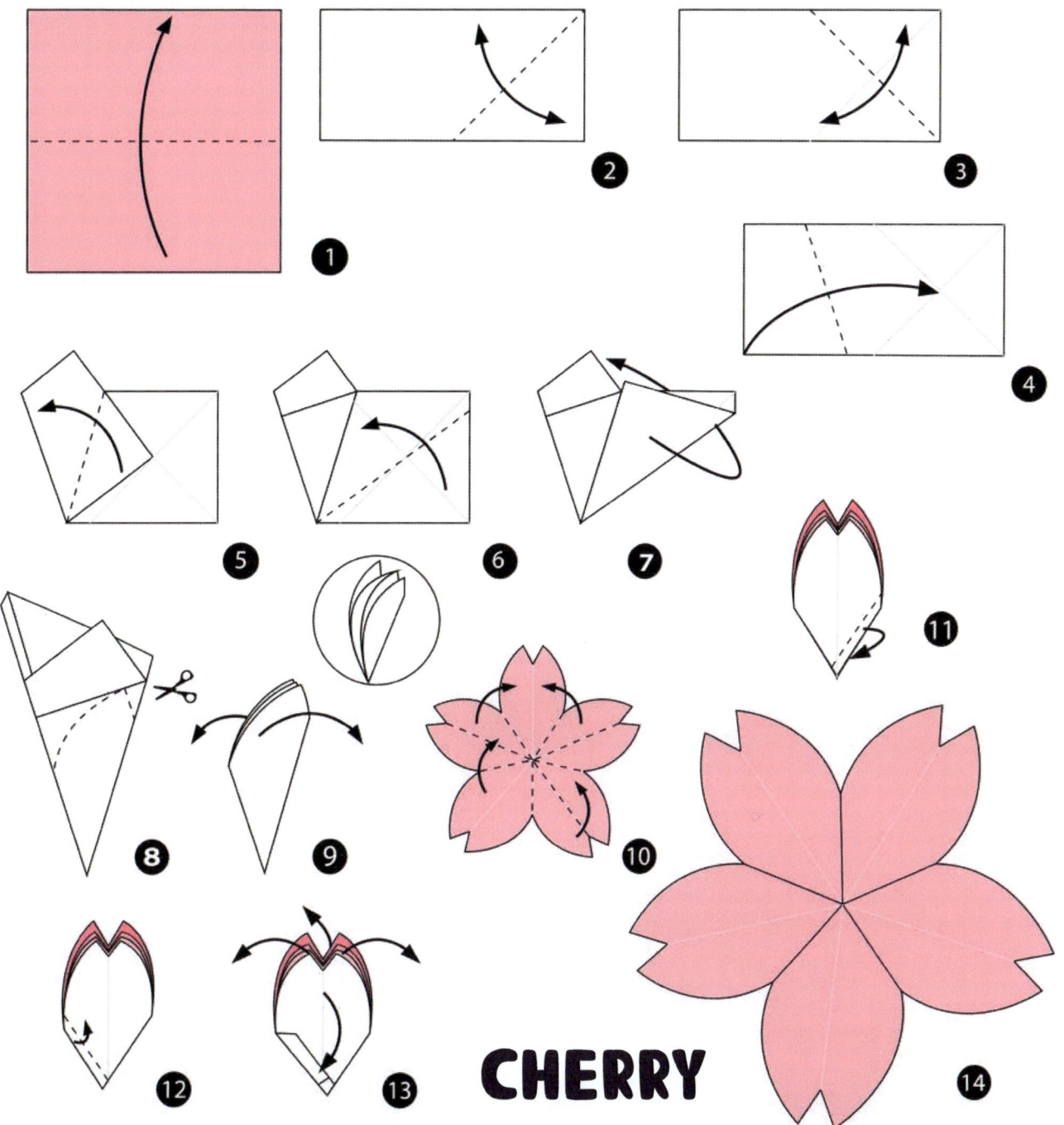
CHERRY

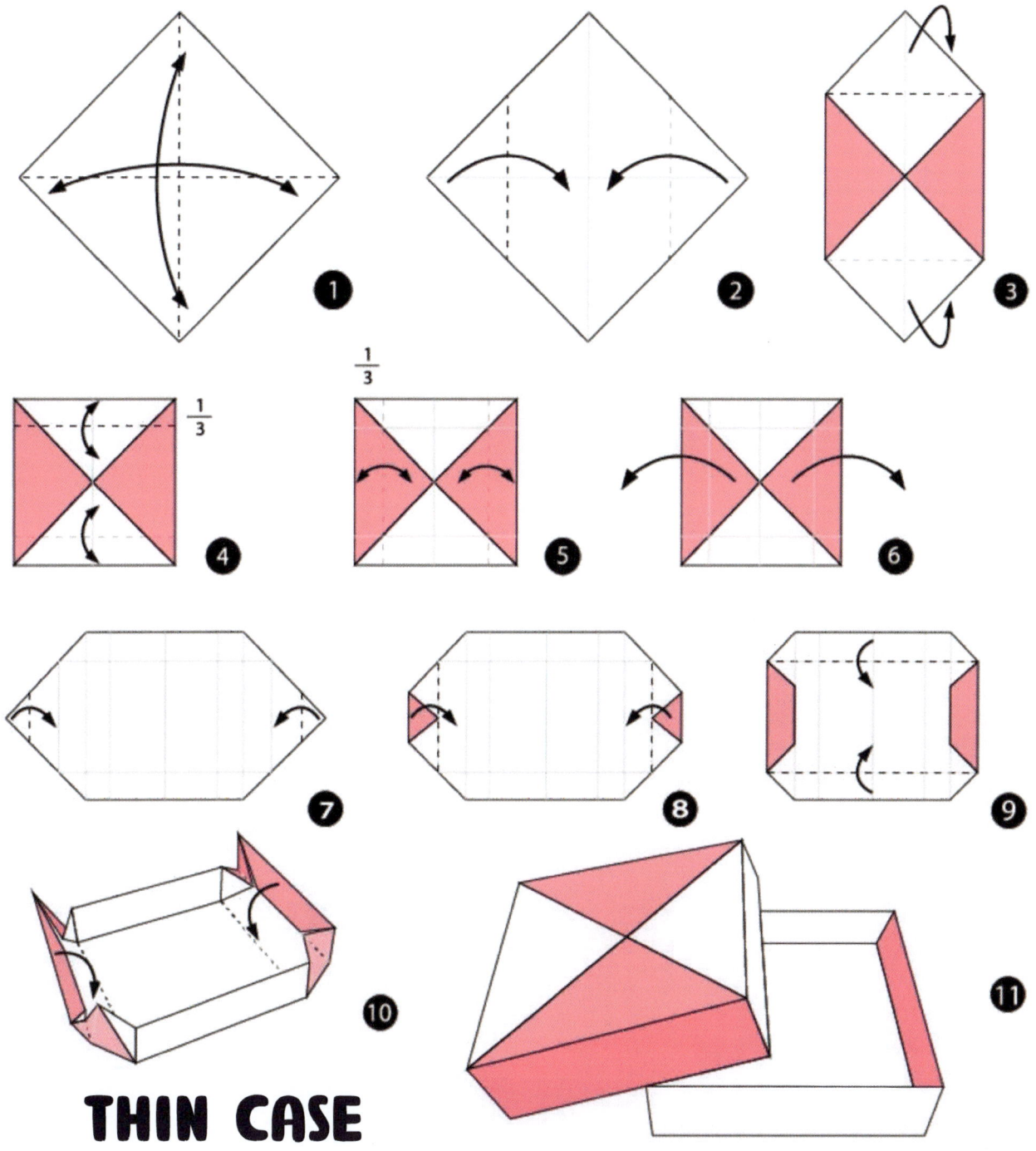

THIN CASE

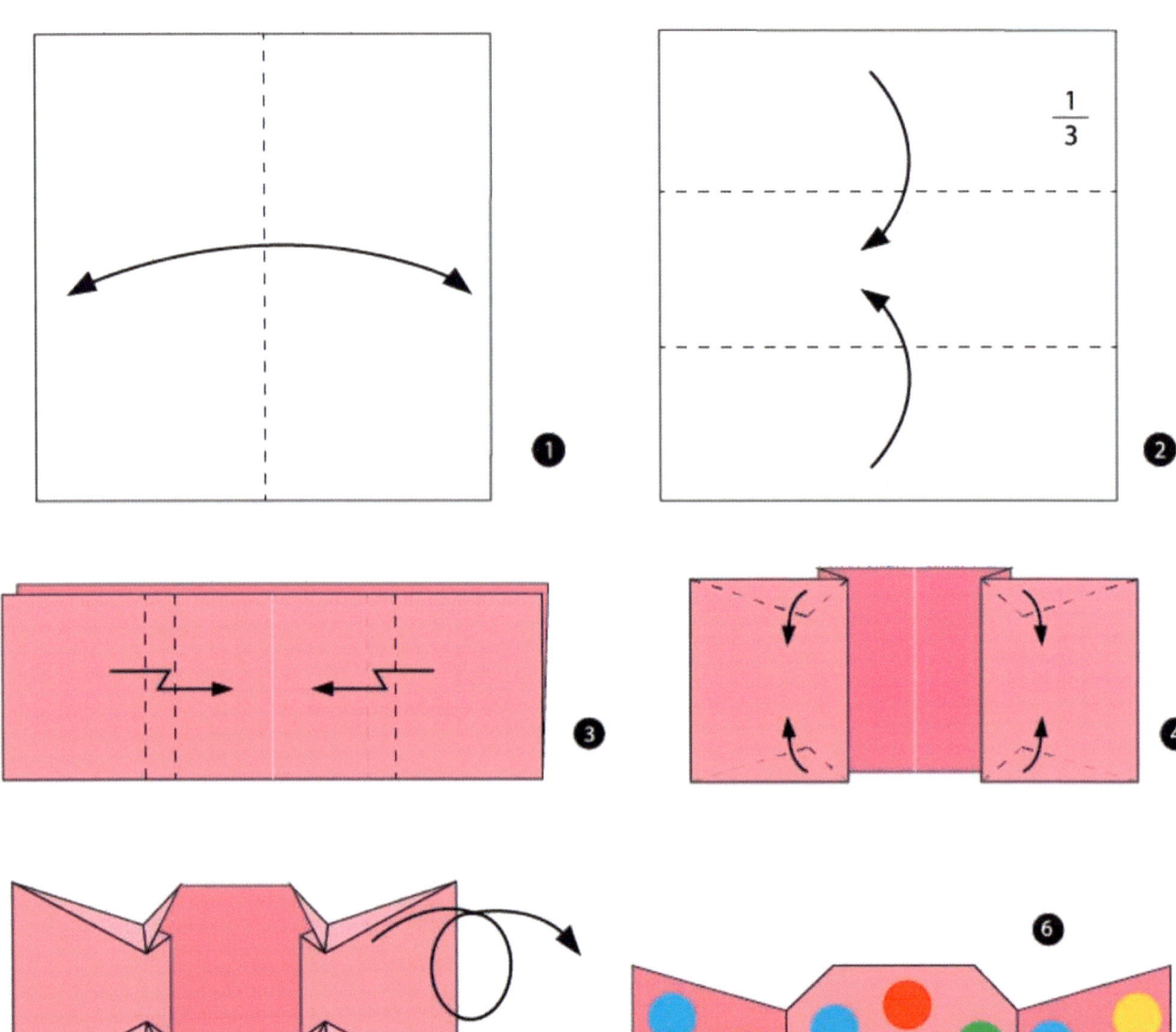

CANDY

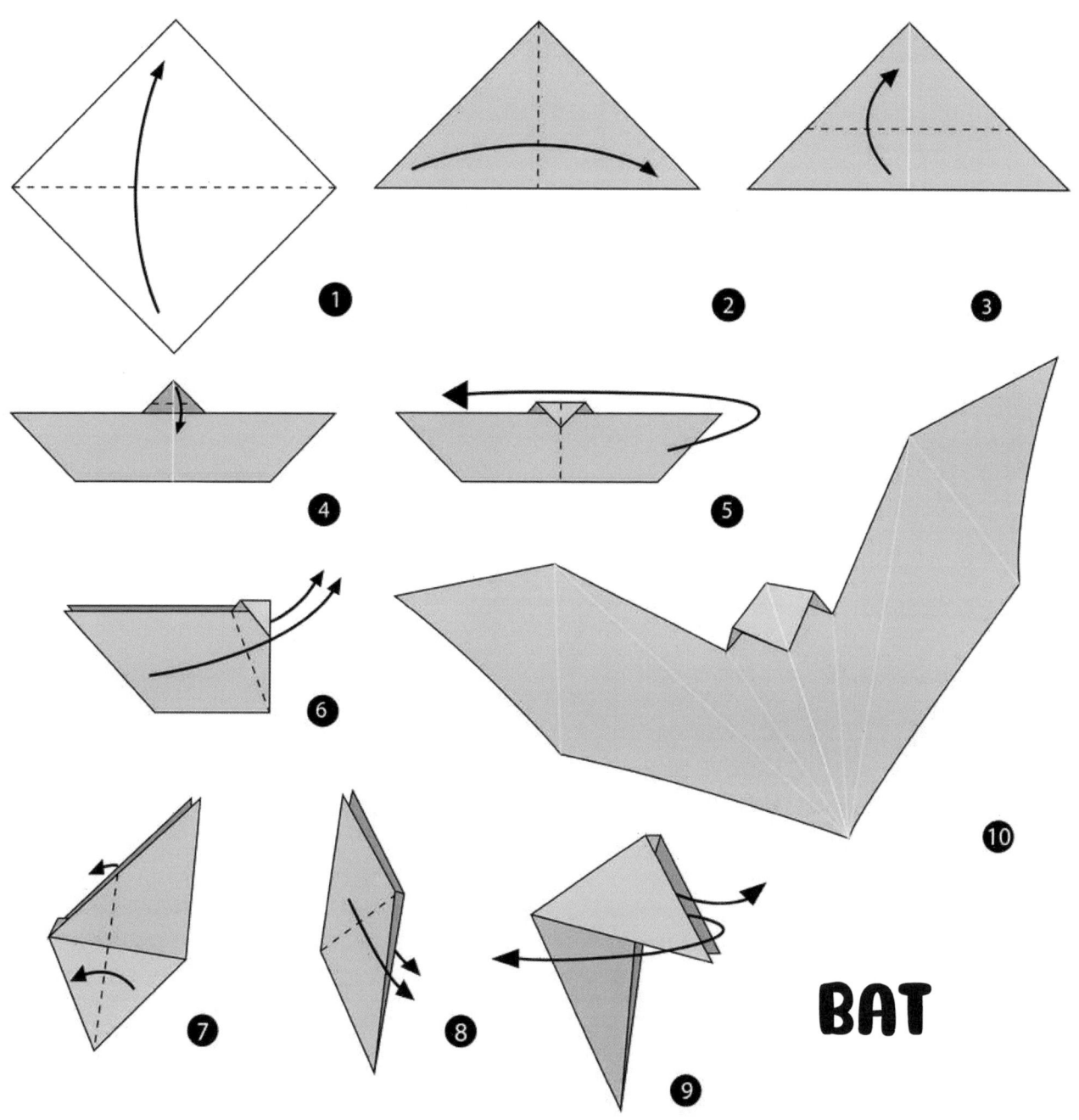

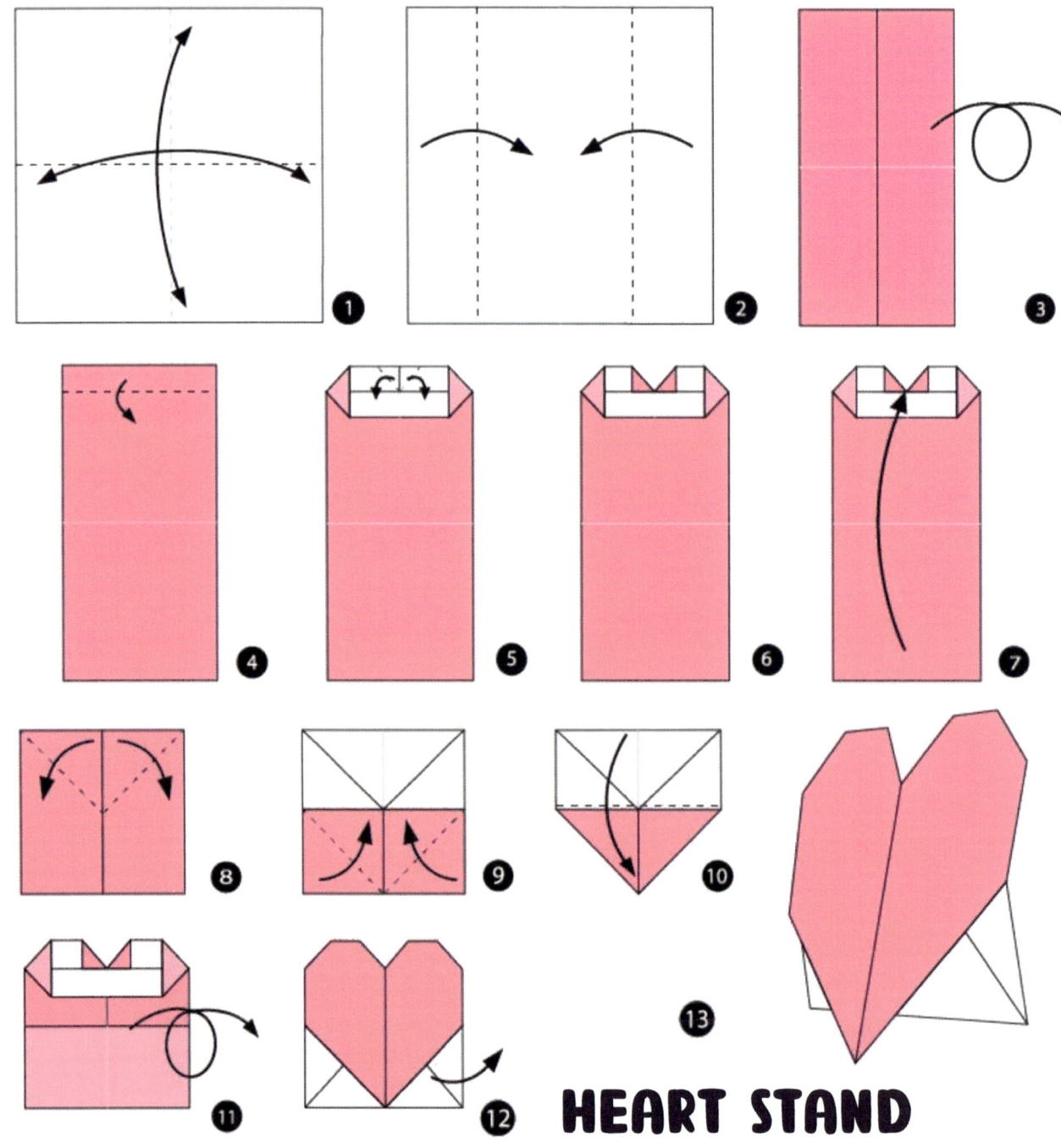

HEART STAND

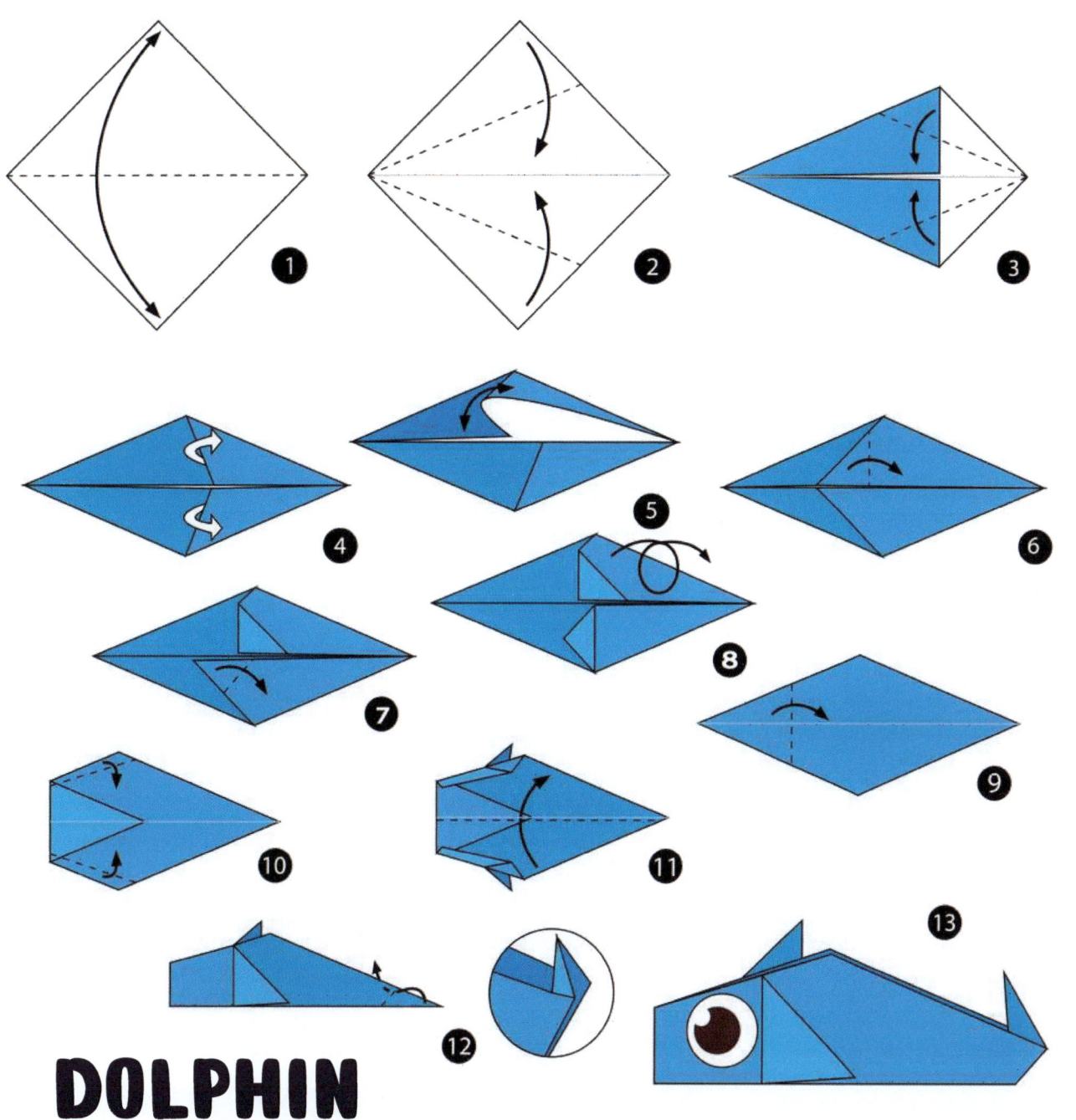

DOLPHIN

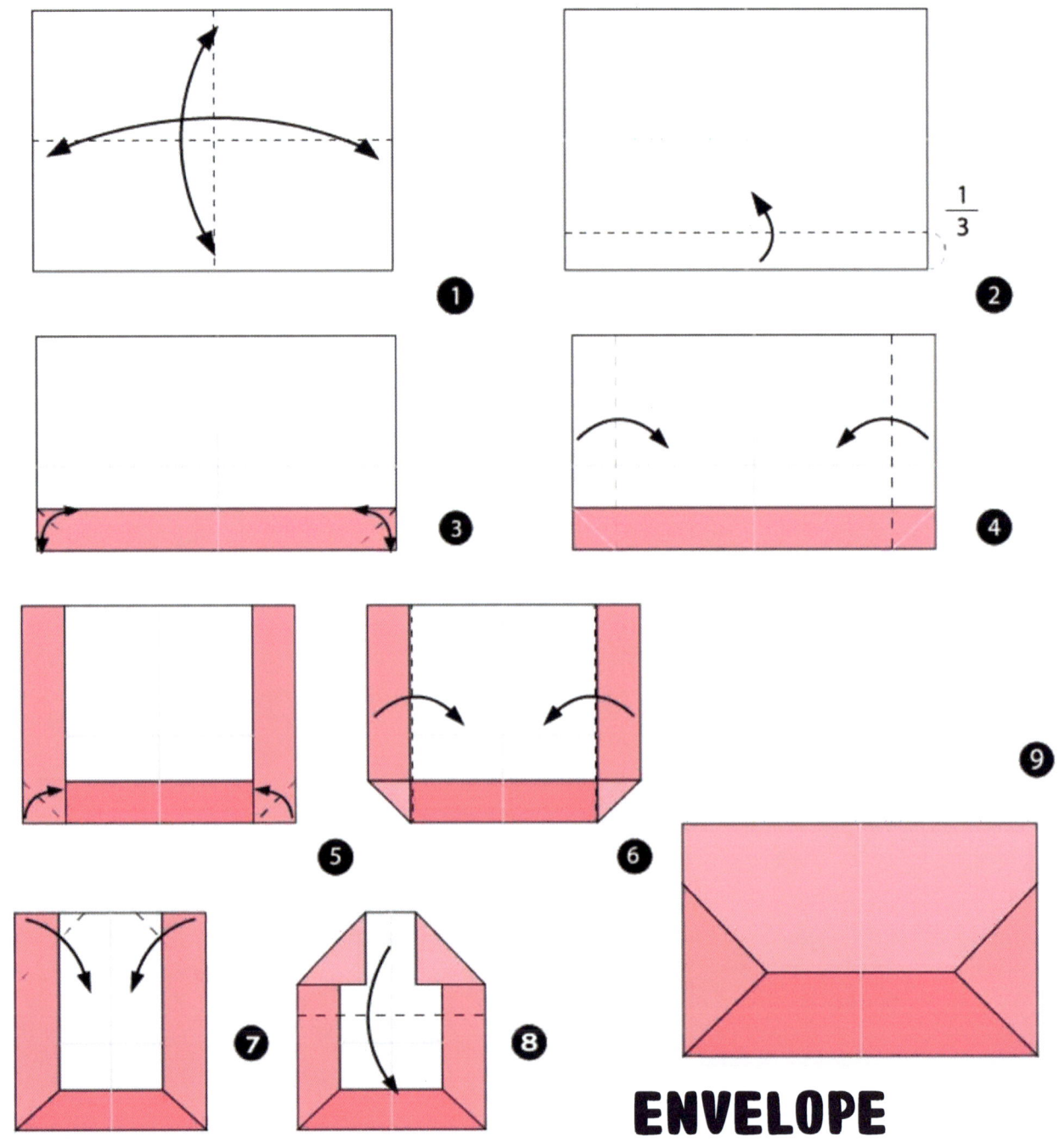

ENVELOPE

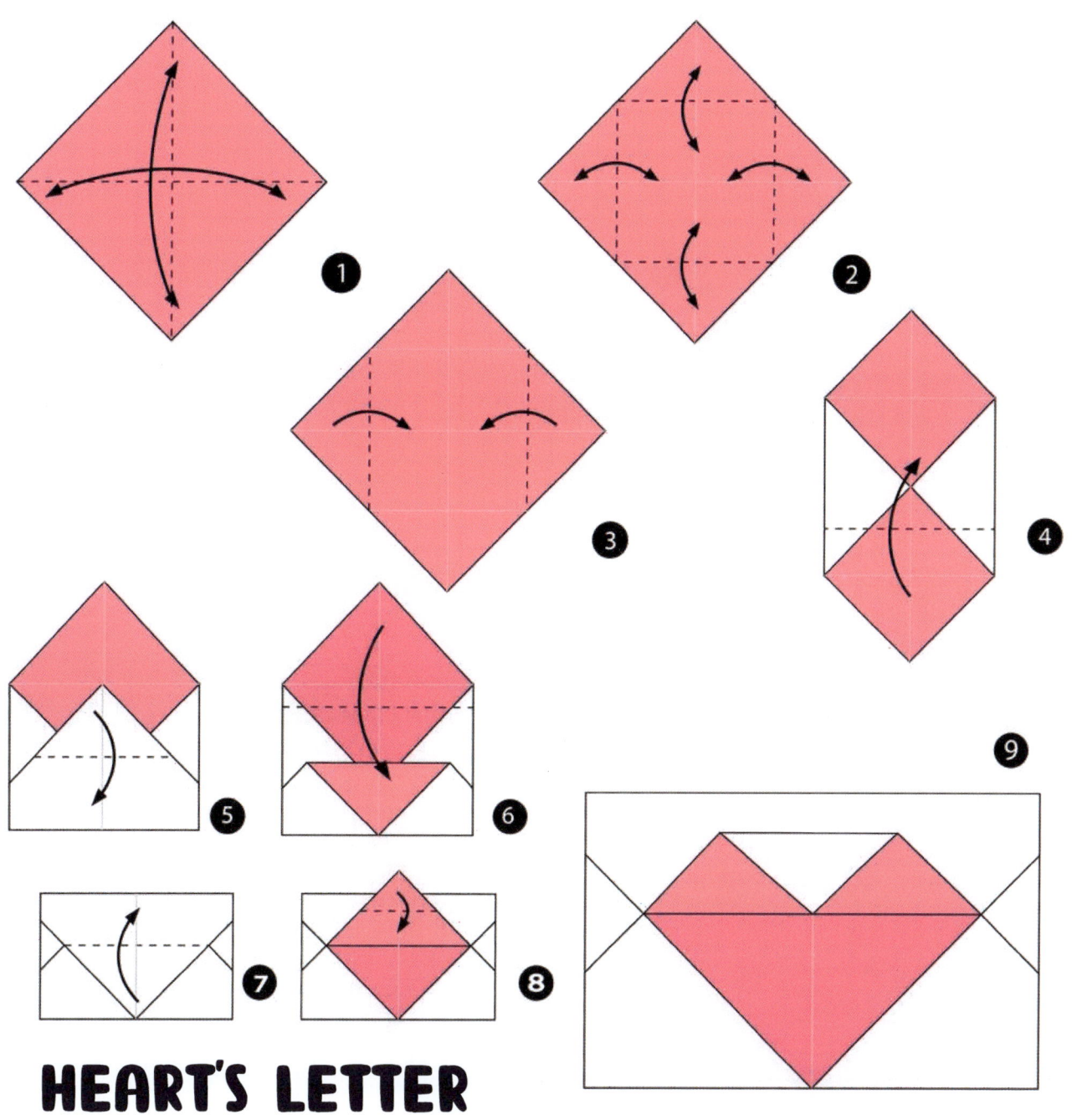

HEART'S LETTER

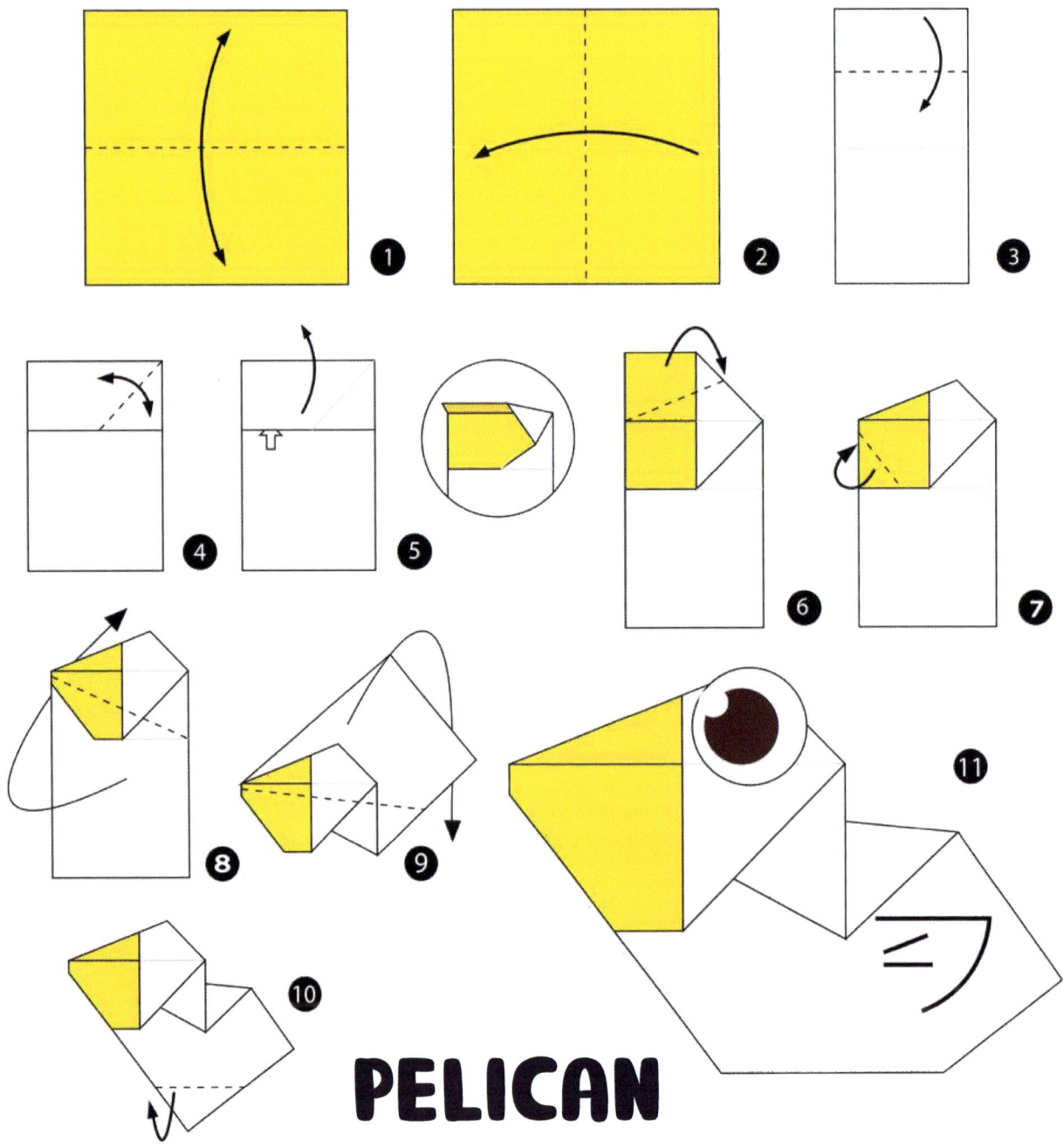

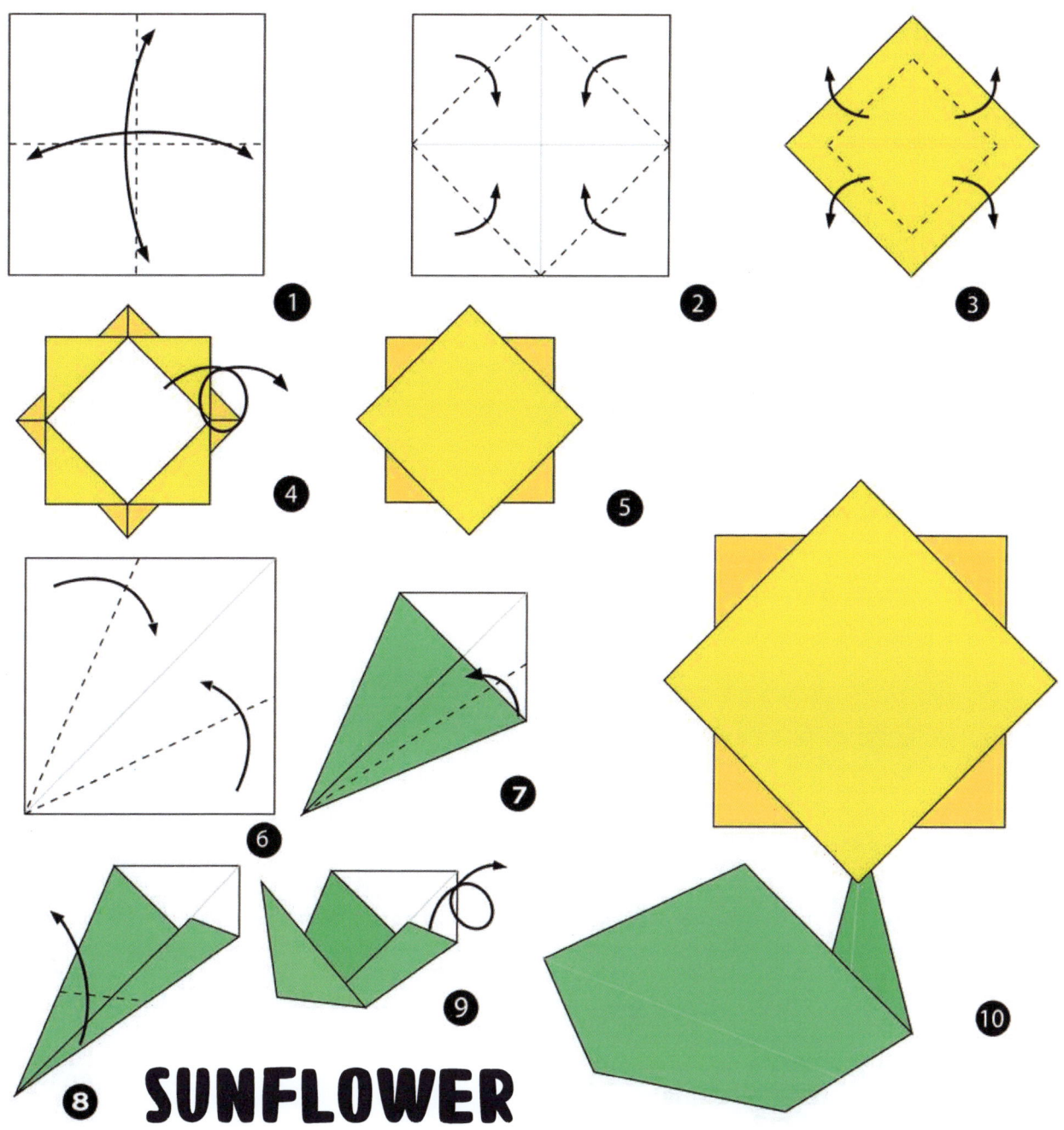

Printed in Great Britain
by Amazon